Life on the Ranch
Coloring Book

Copyright © 2012 Deborah S. Huffman

All rights reserved.

ISBN:1978245793
ISBN-13: 9781978245792

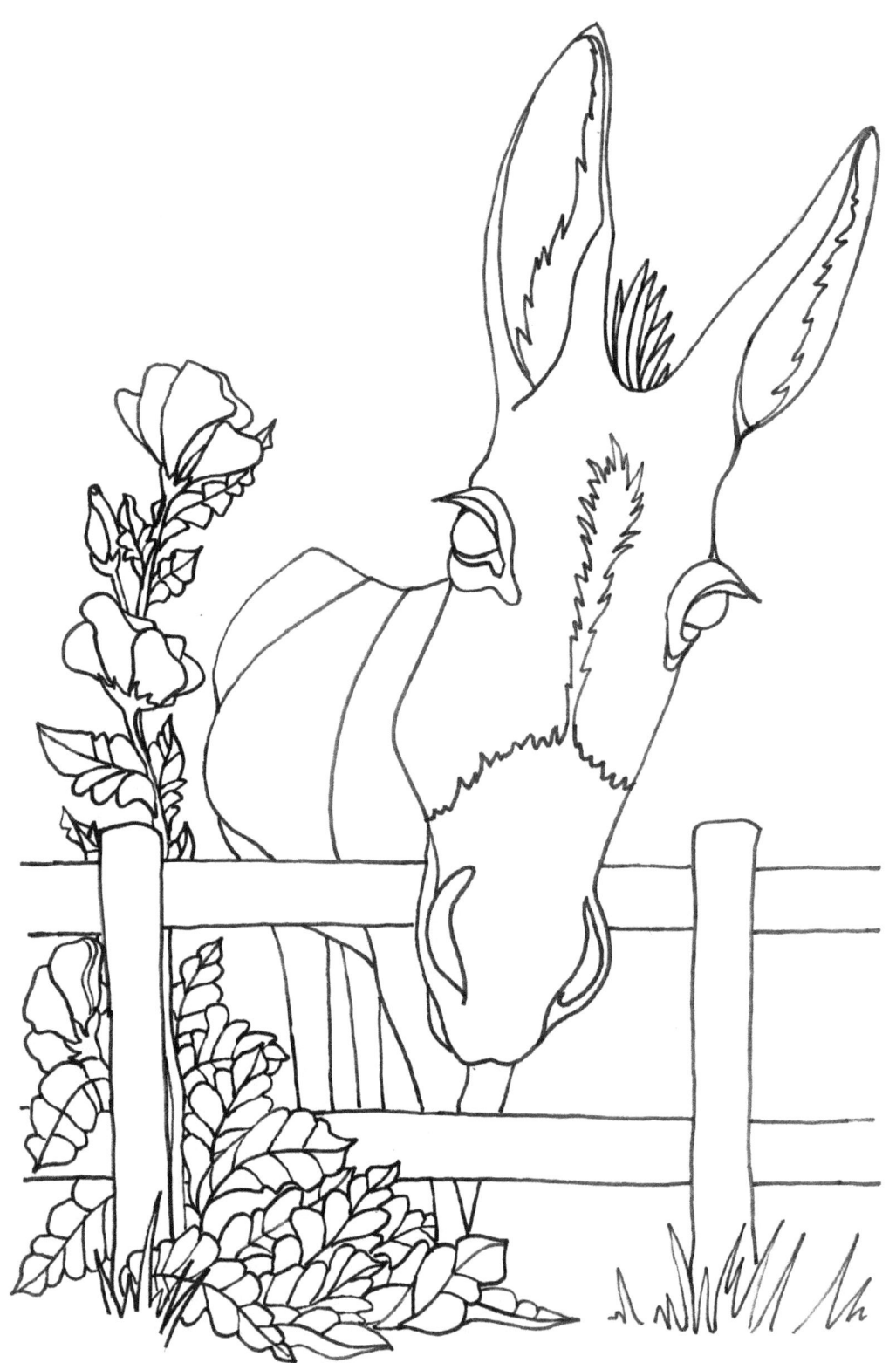

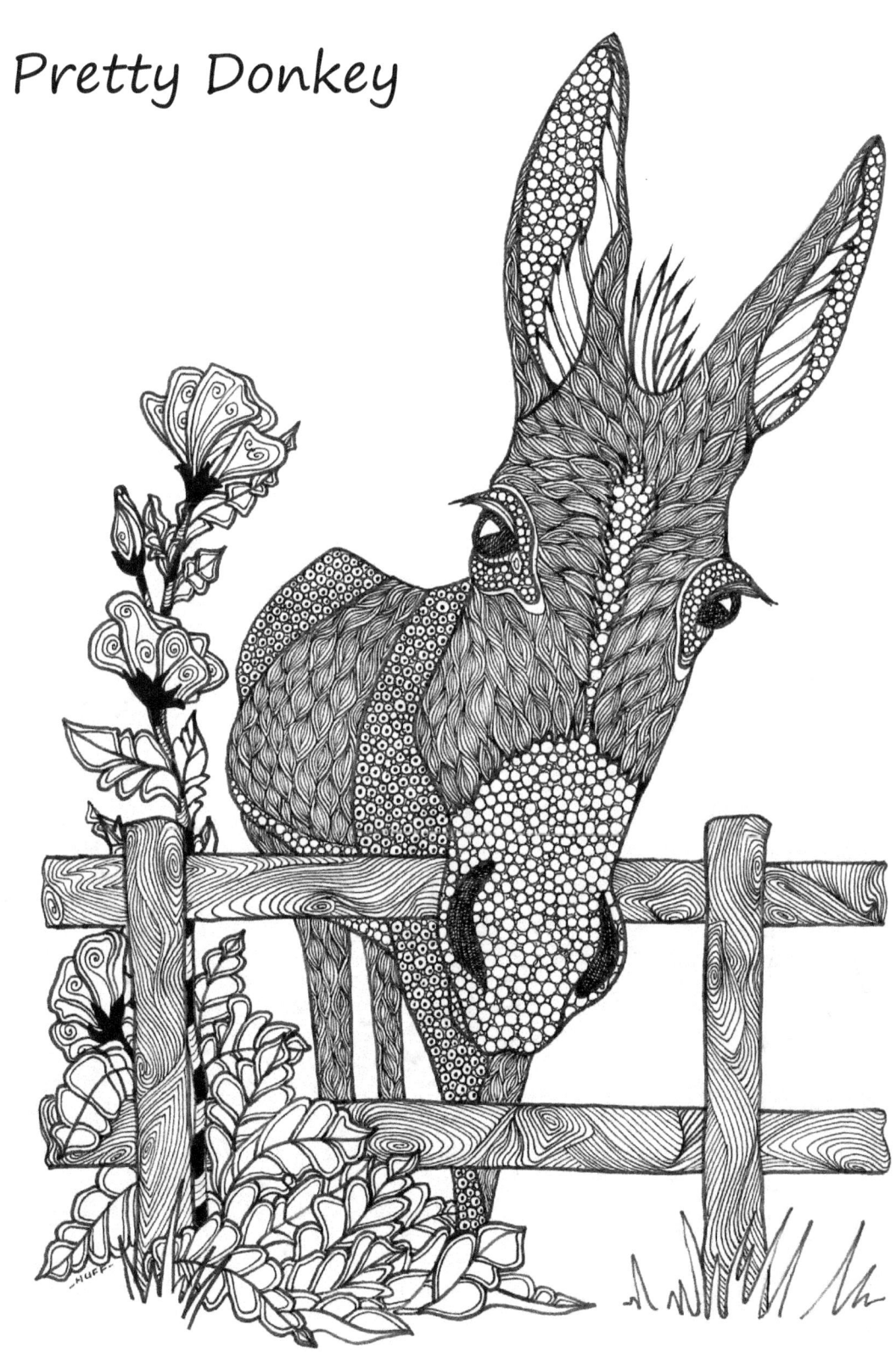

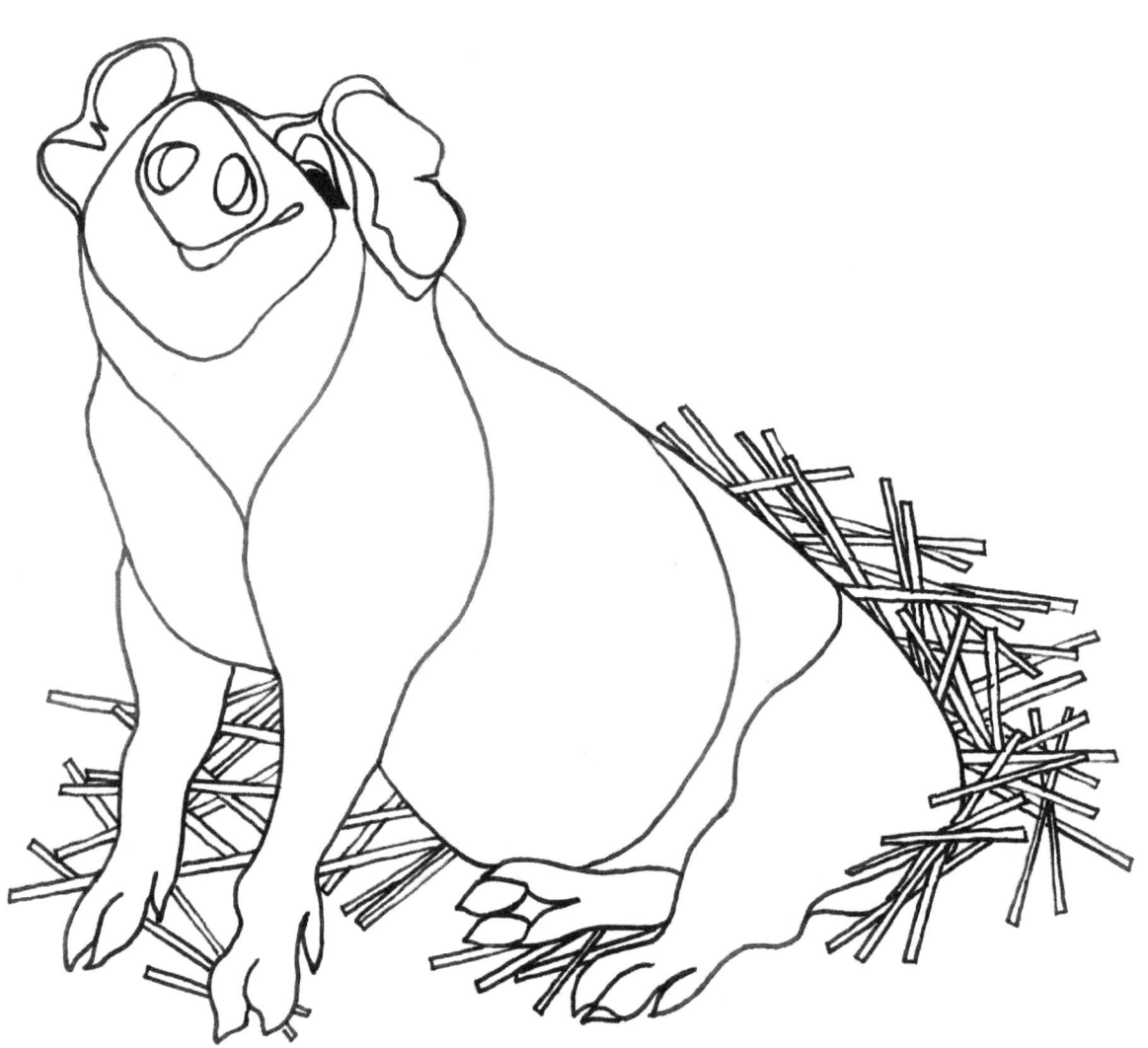

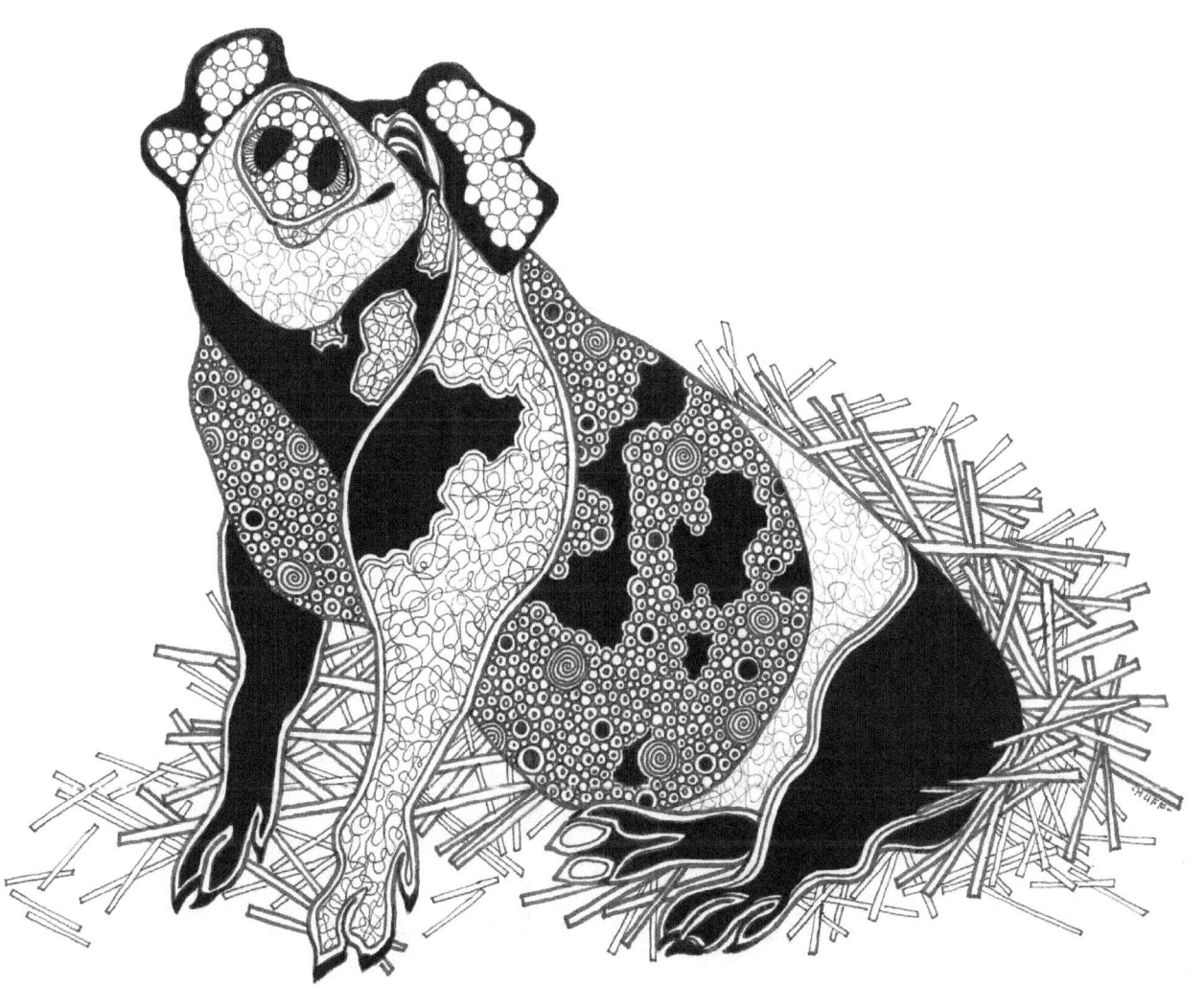

Satisfied Pig

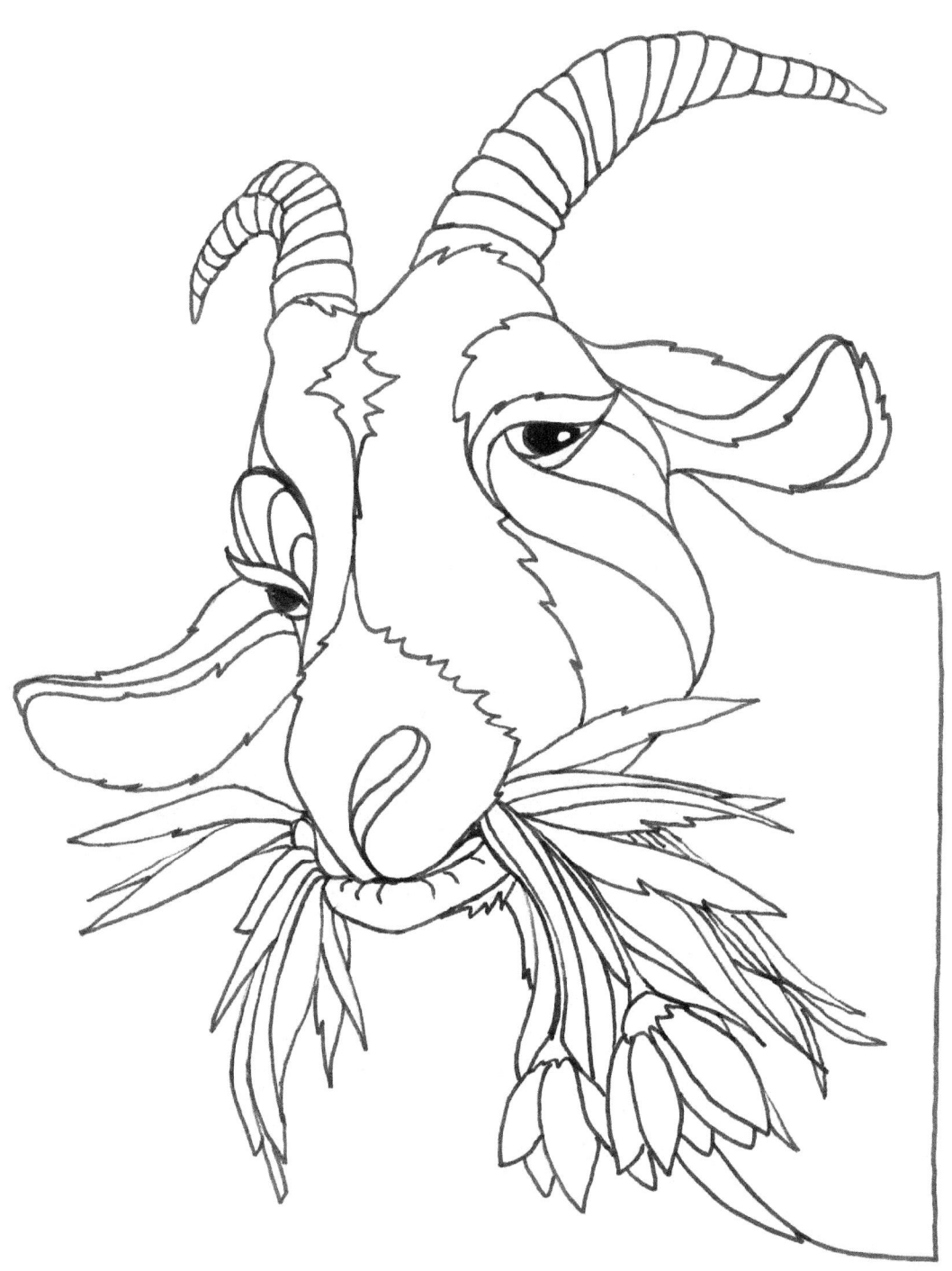

Munching Goat

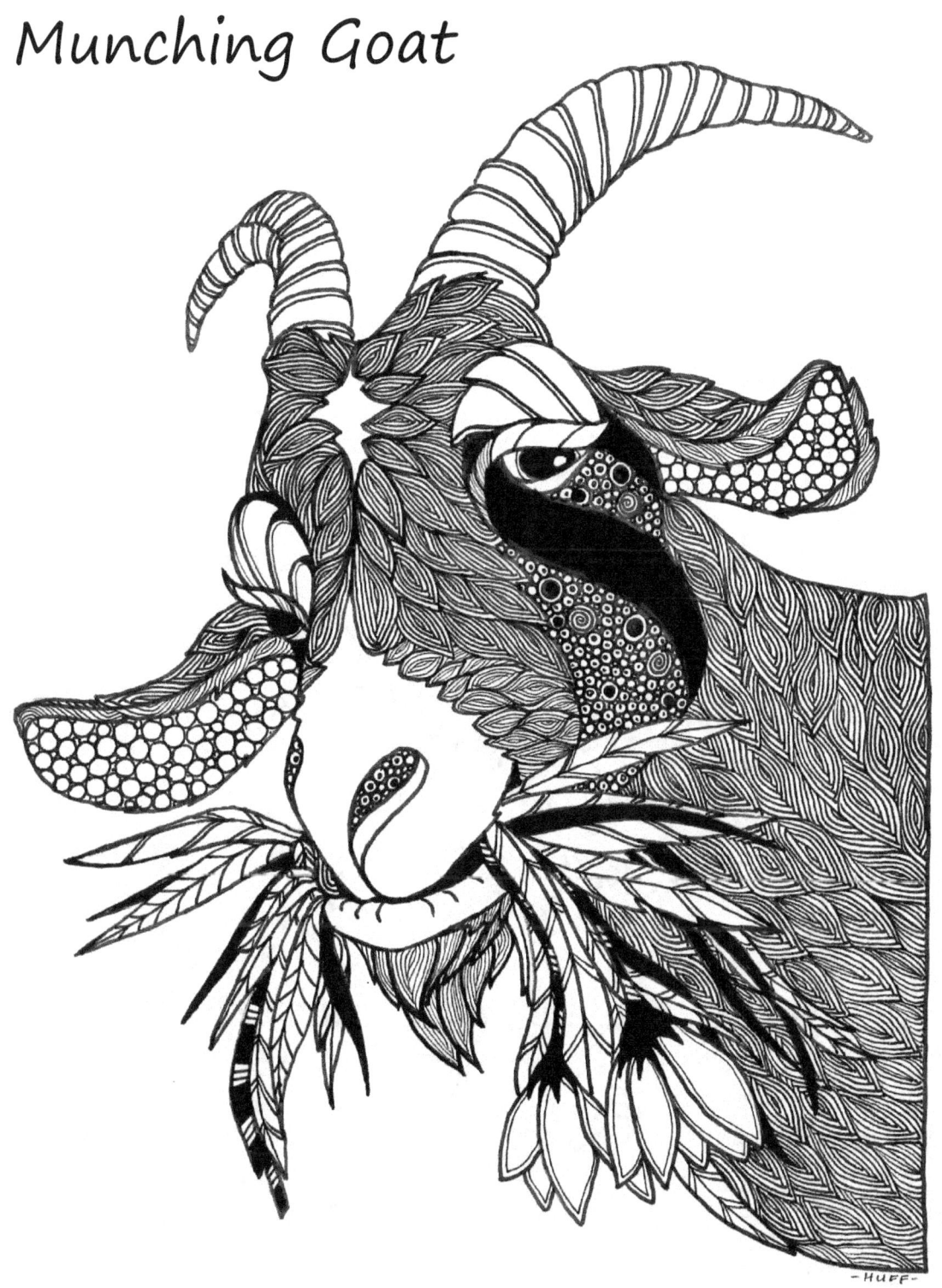

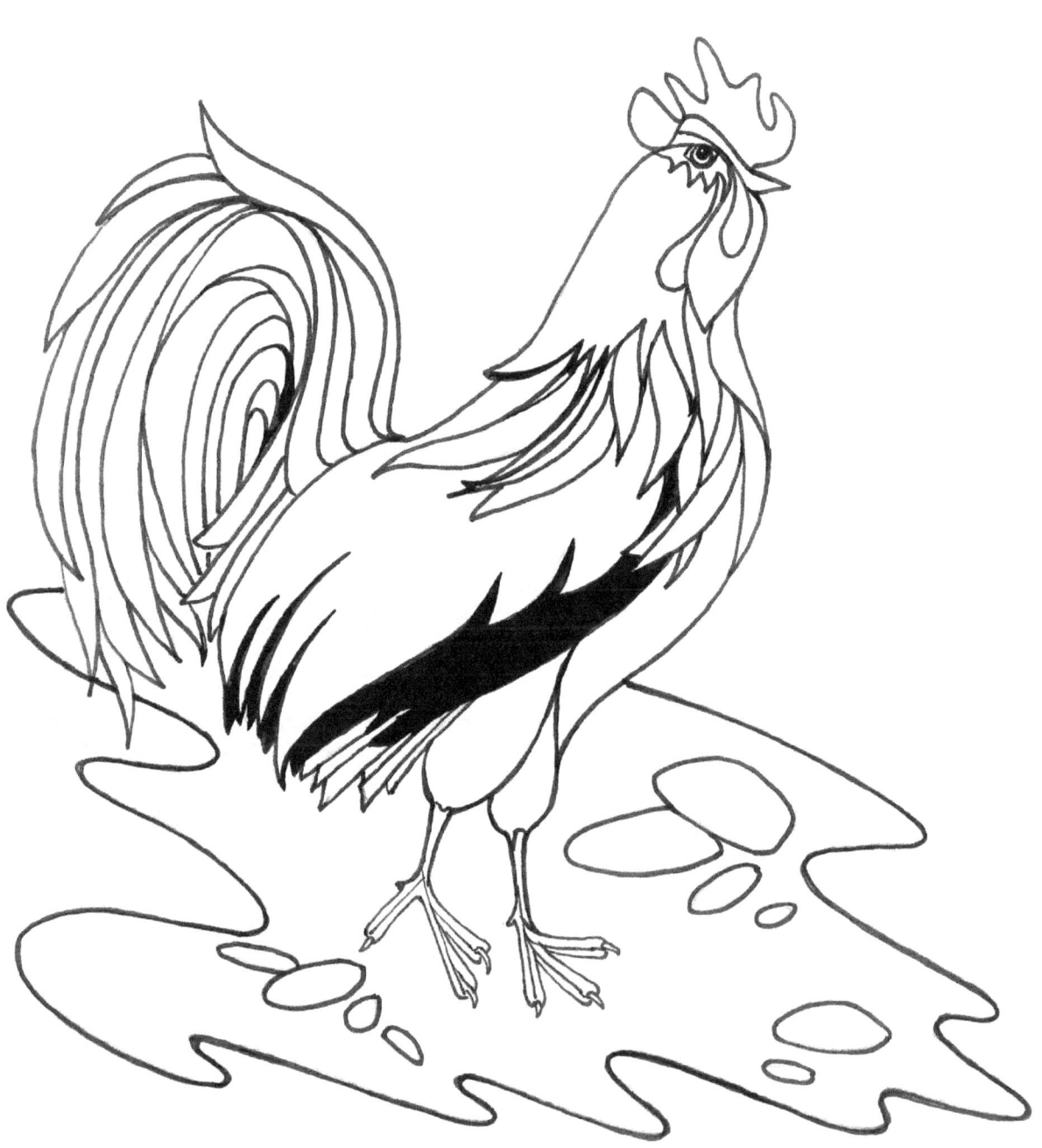

Strutting Rooster

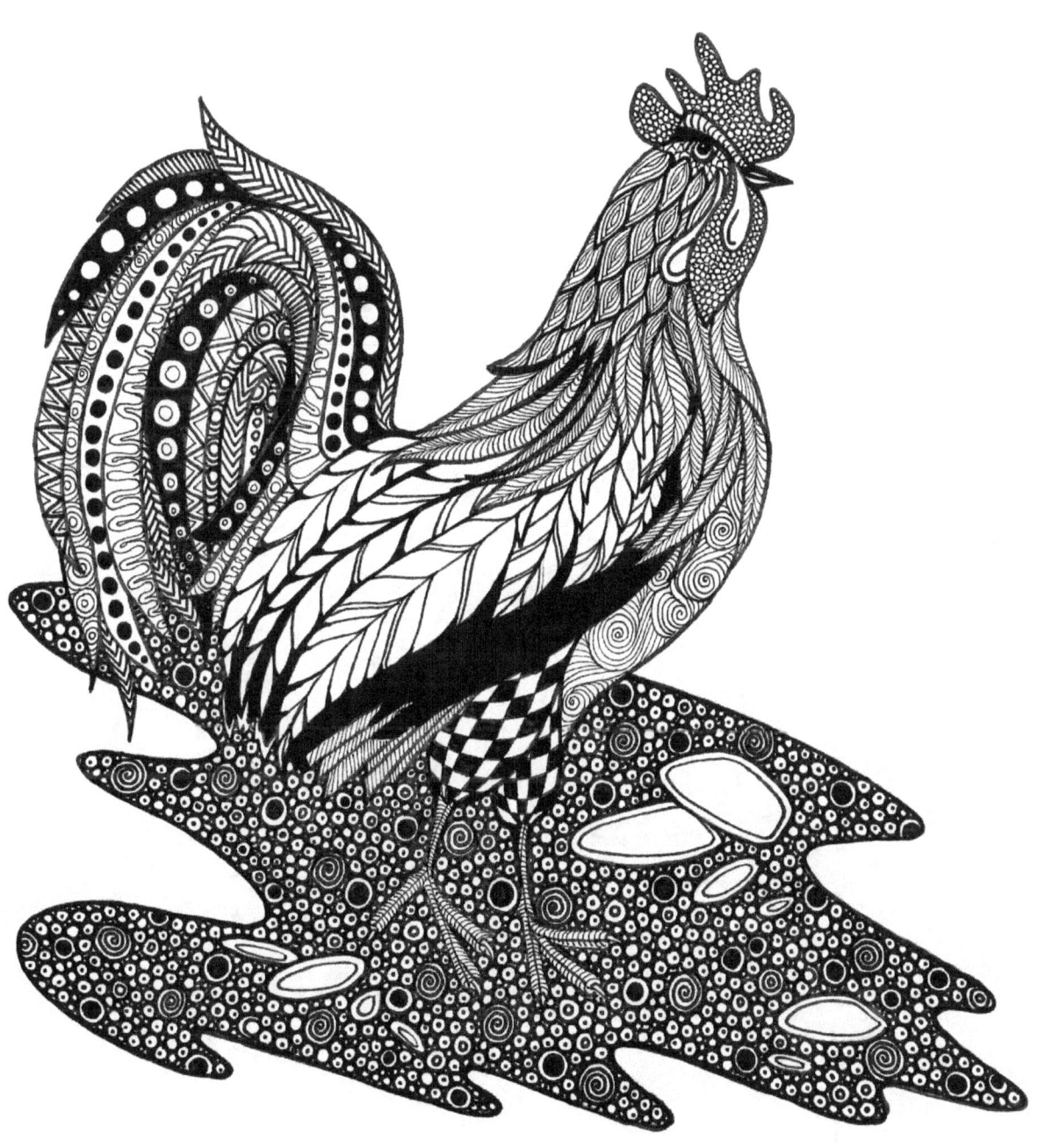

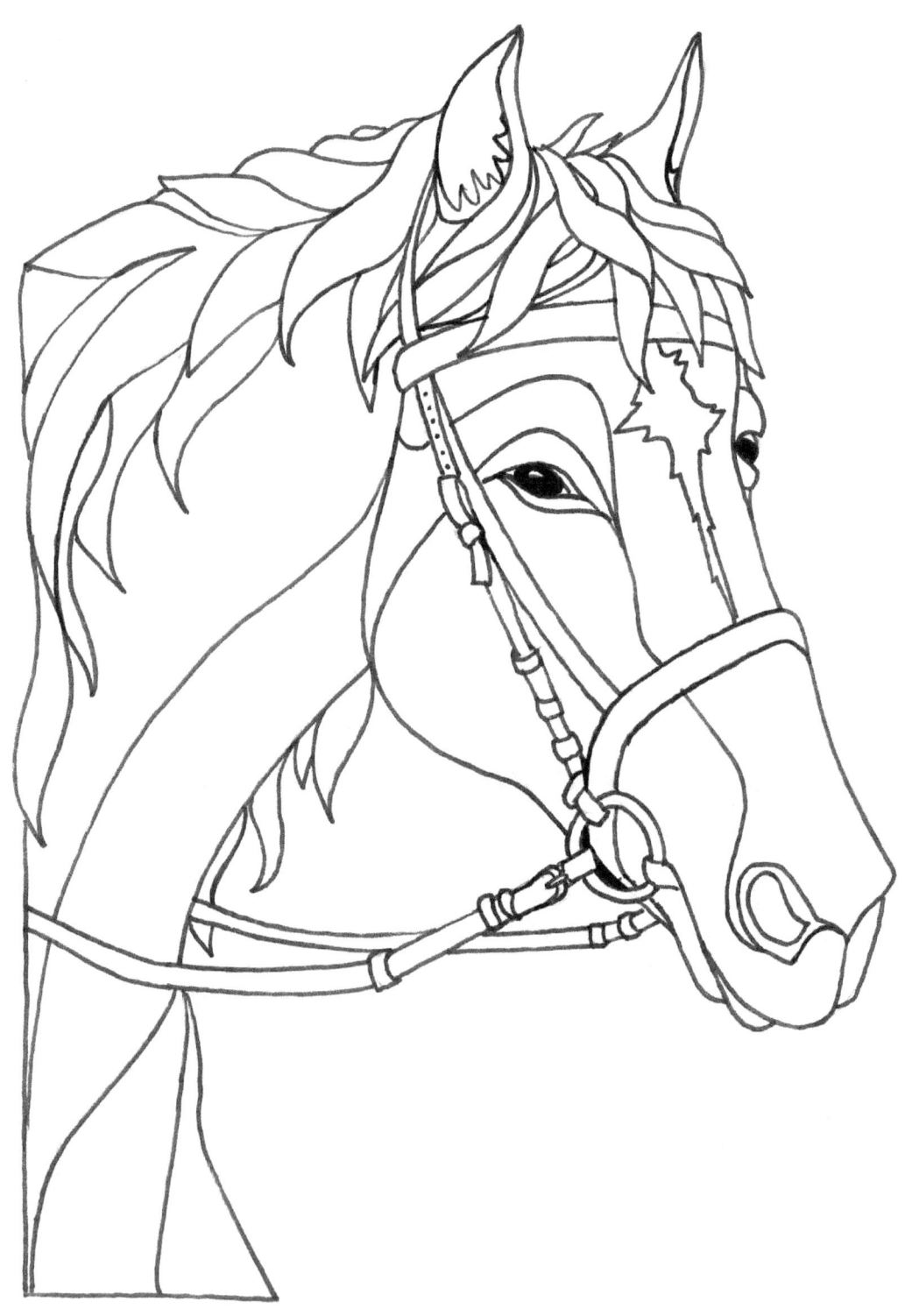

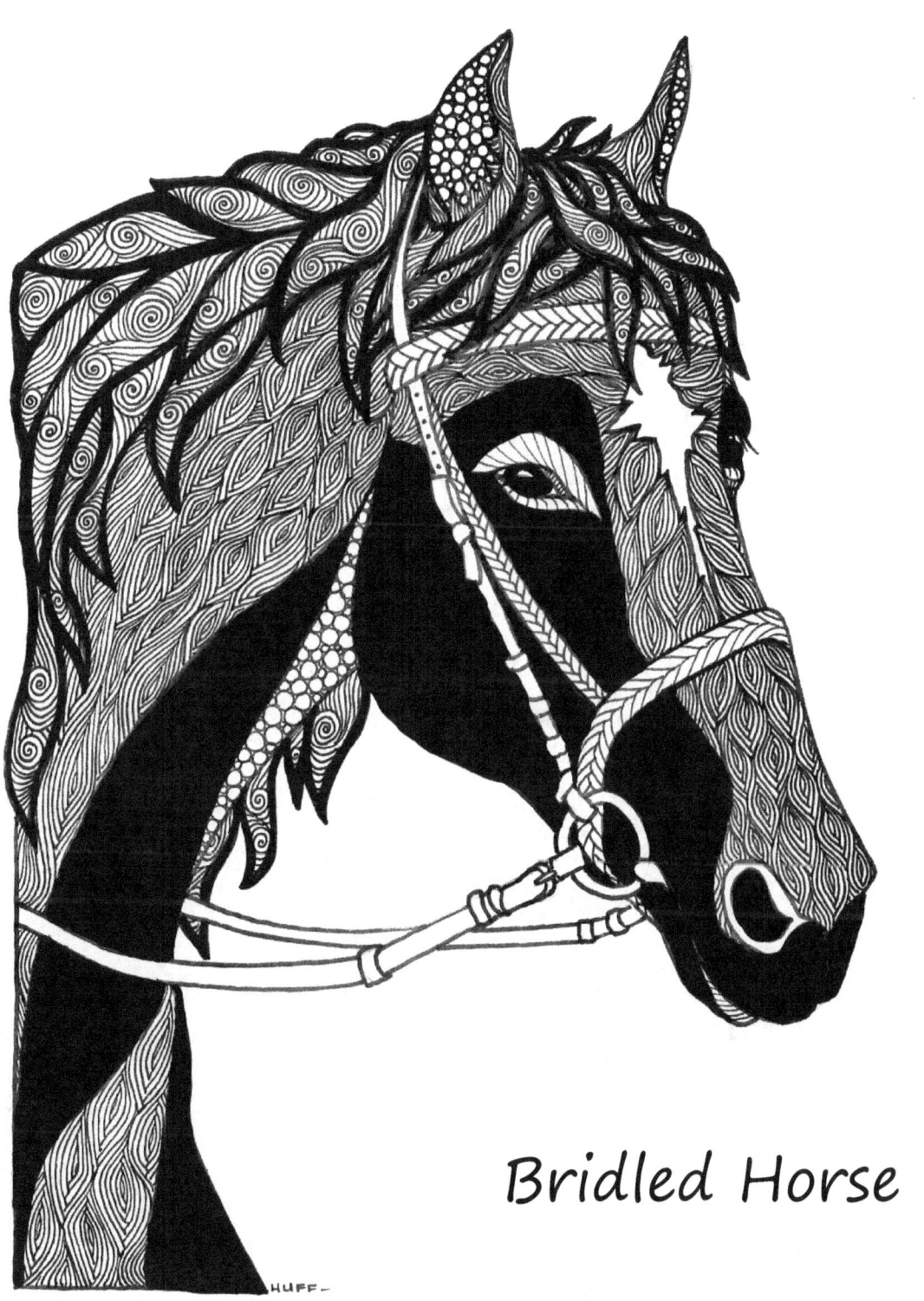

Bridled Horse

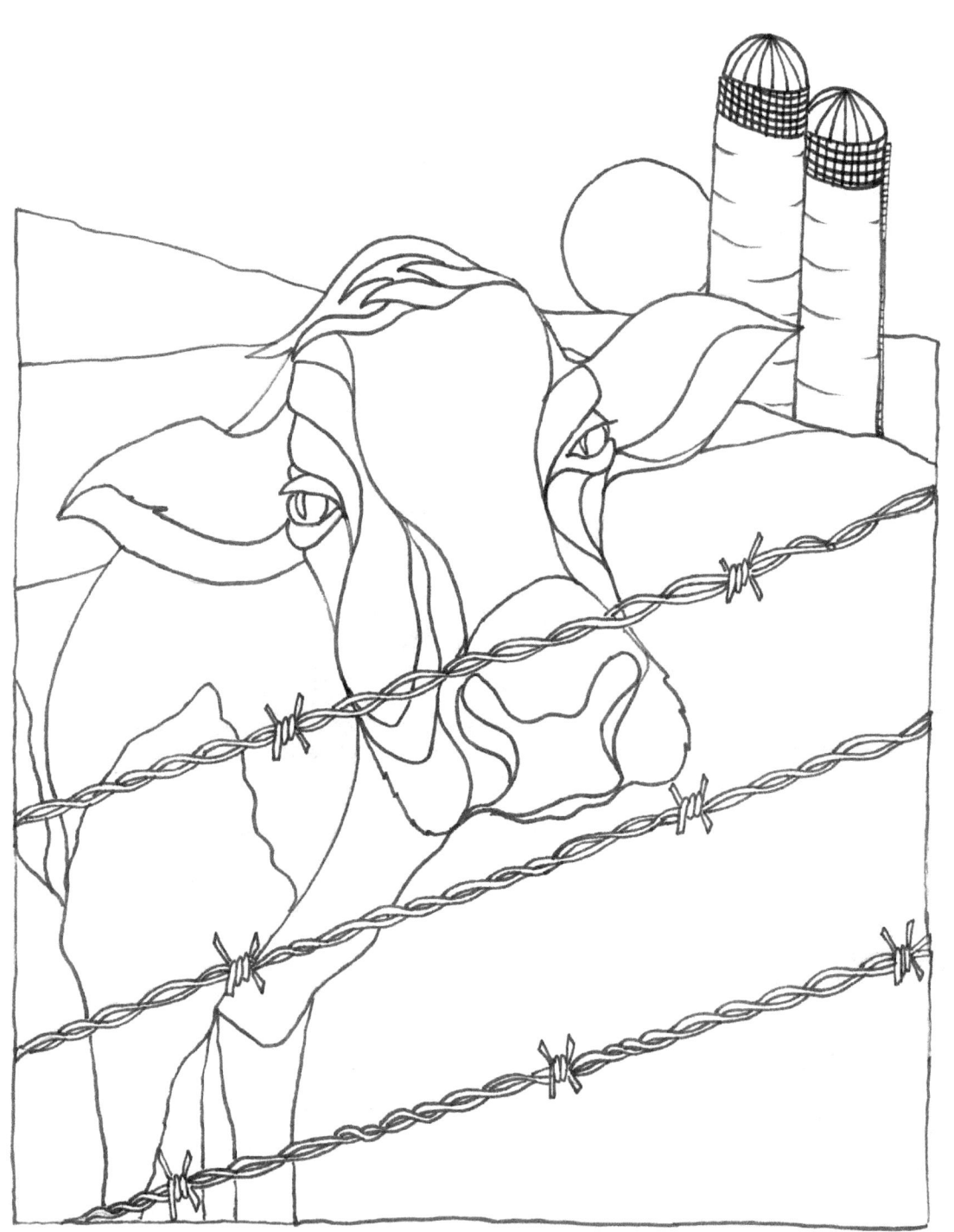

Calm Cow

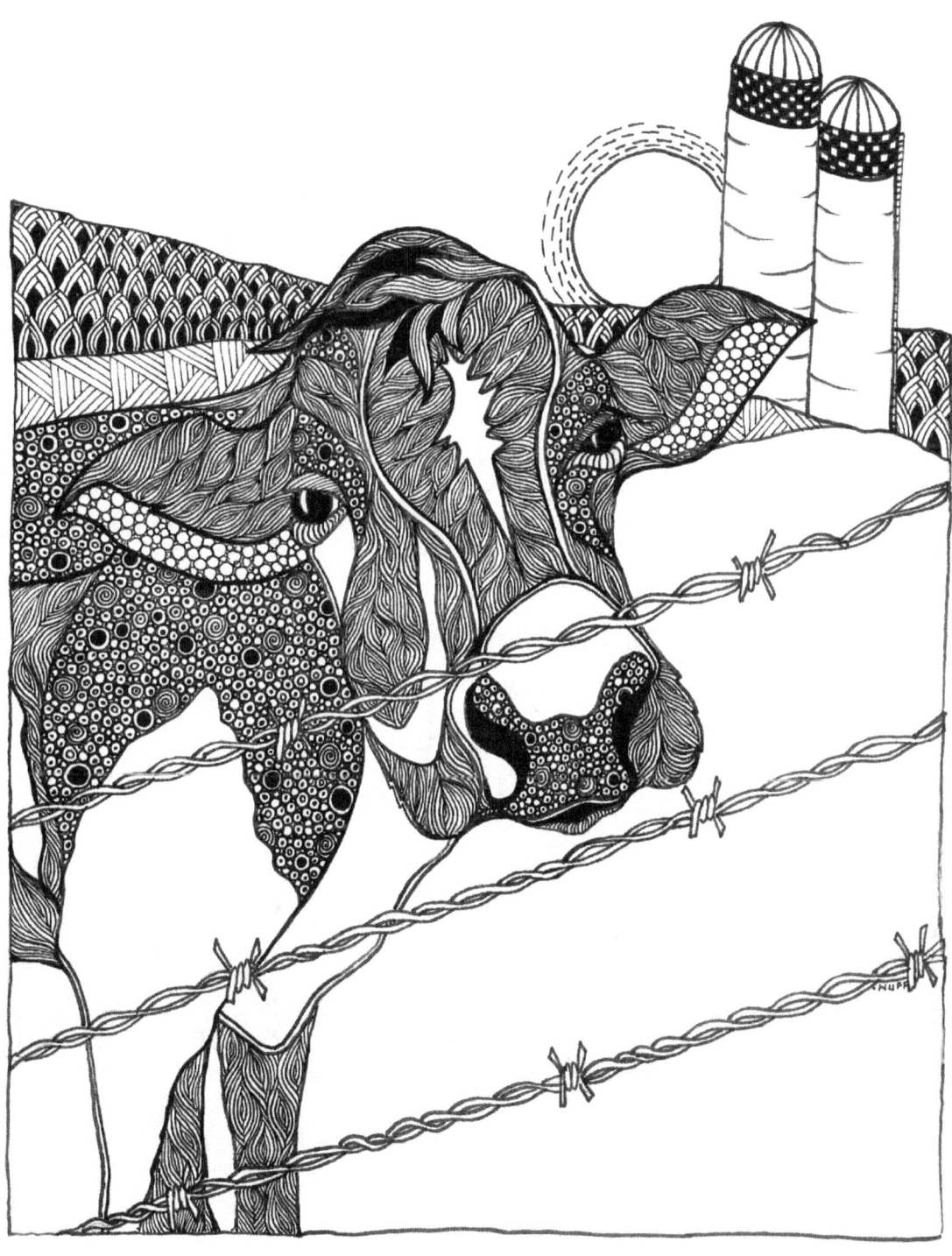

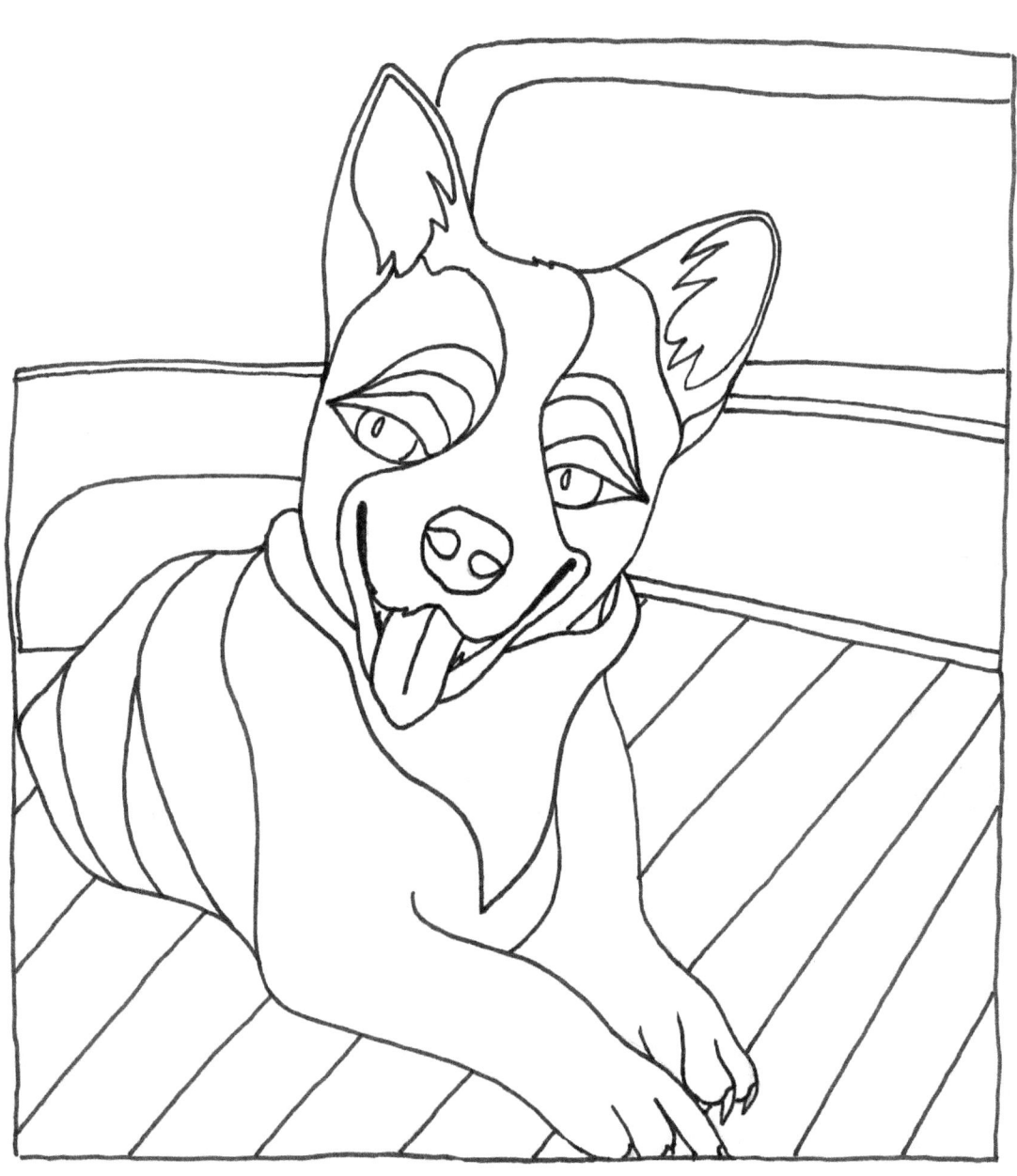

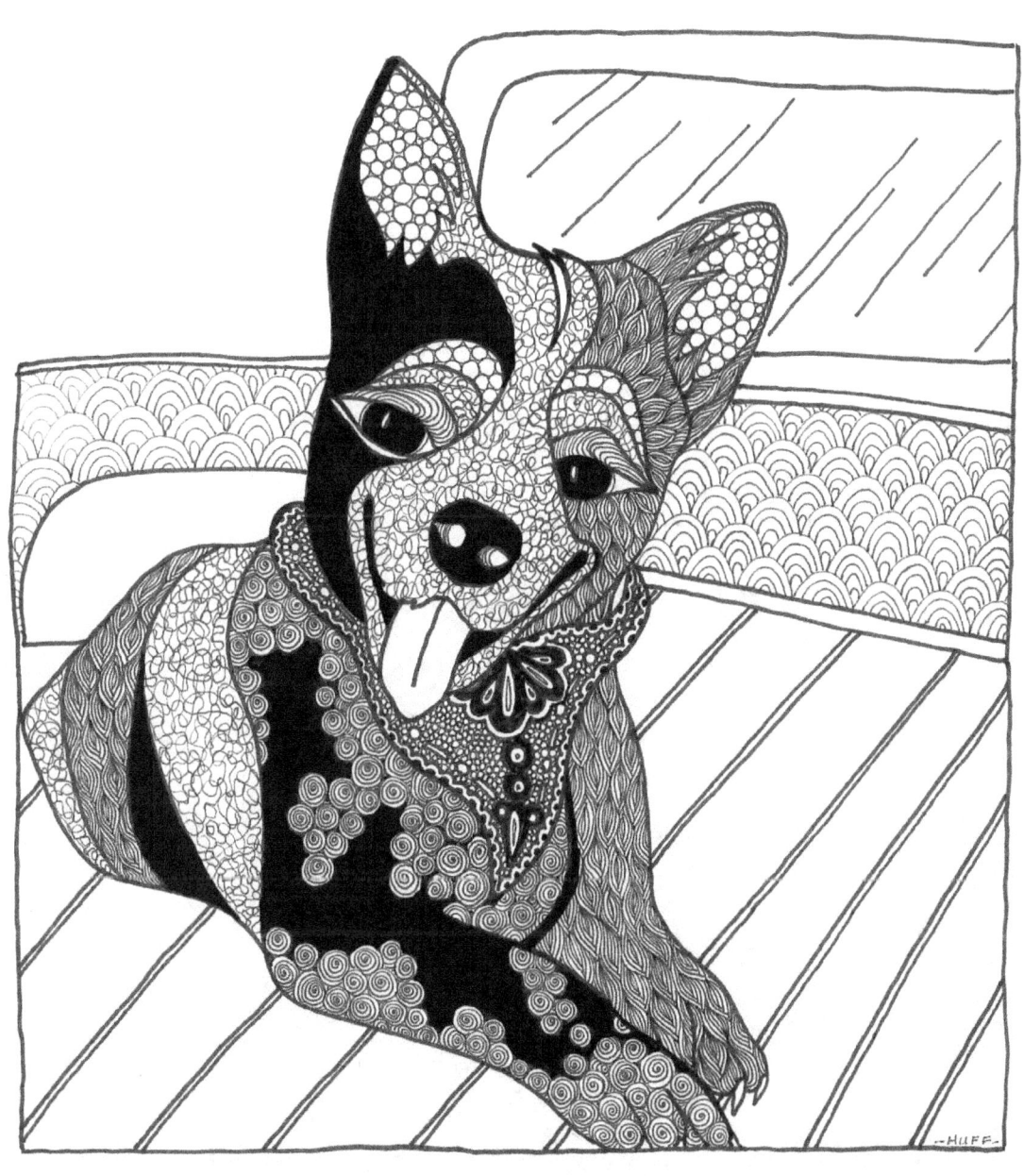

Pup in a Truck

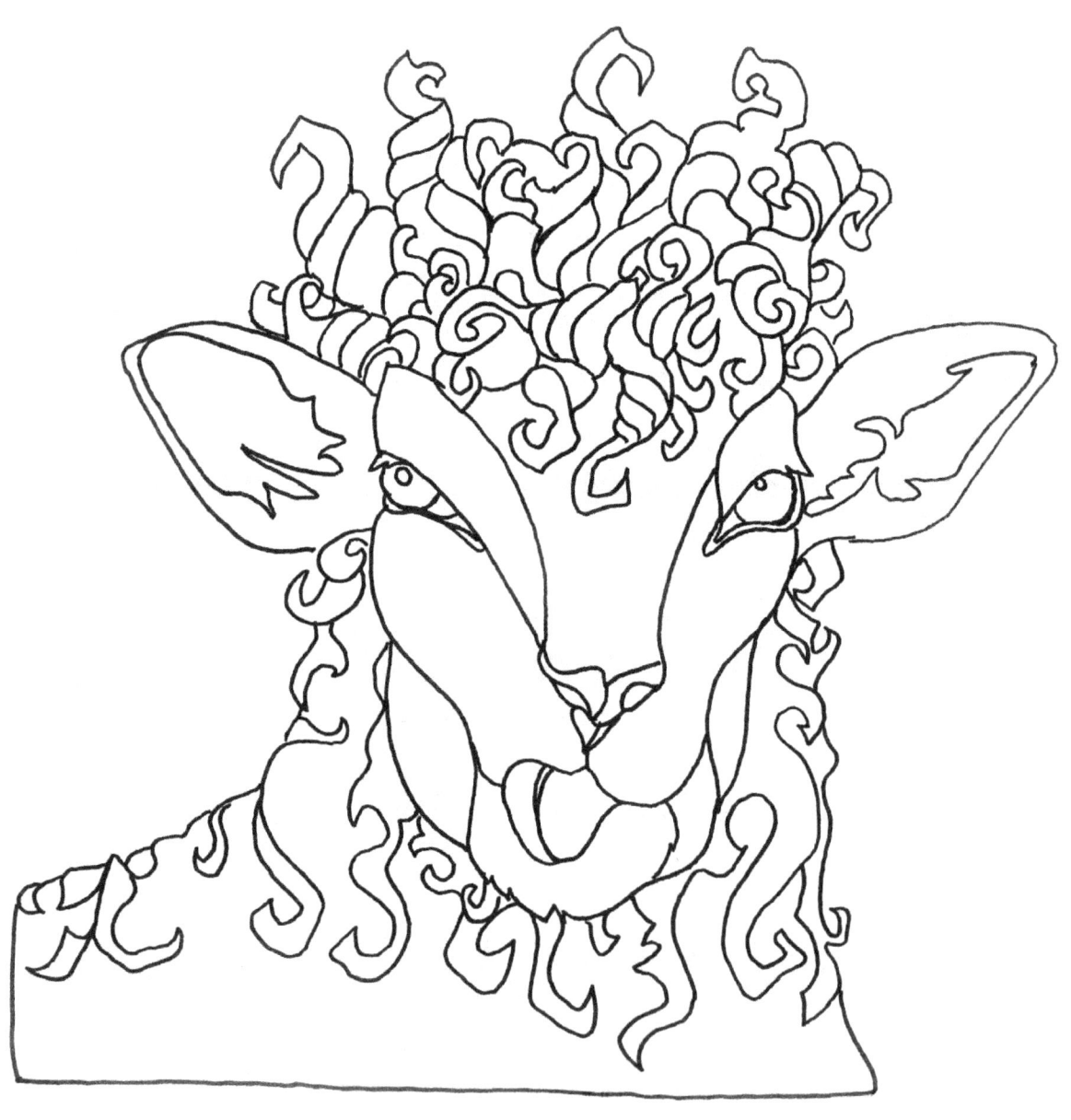

Curly Sheep

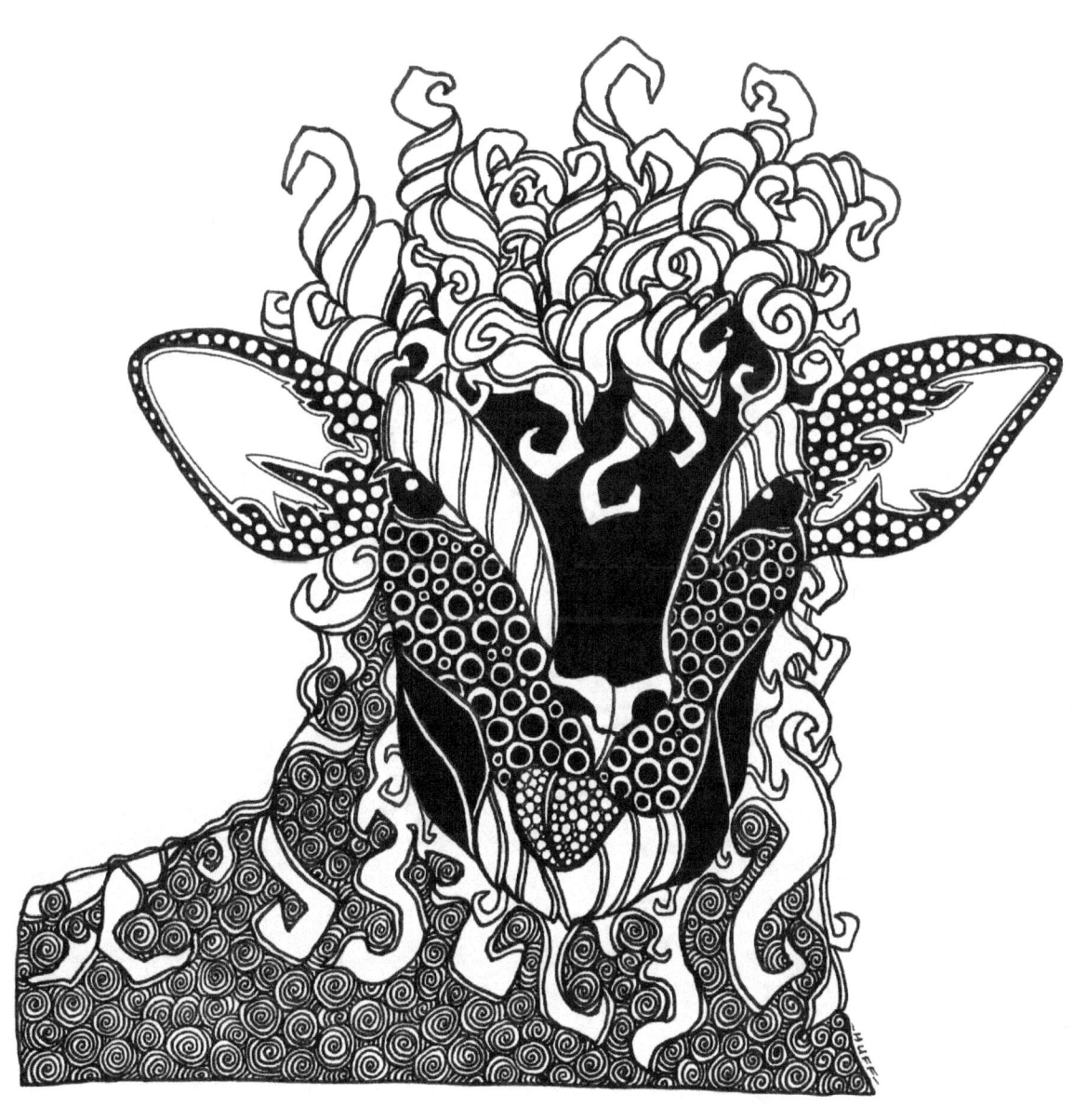

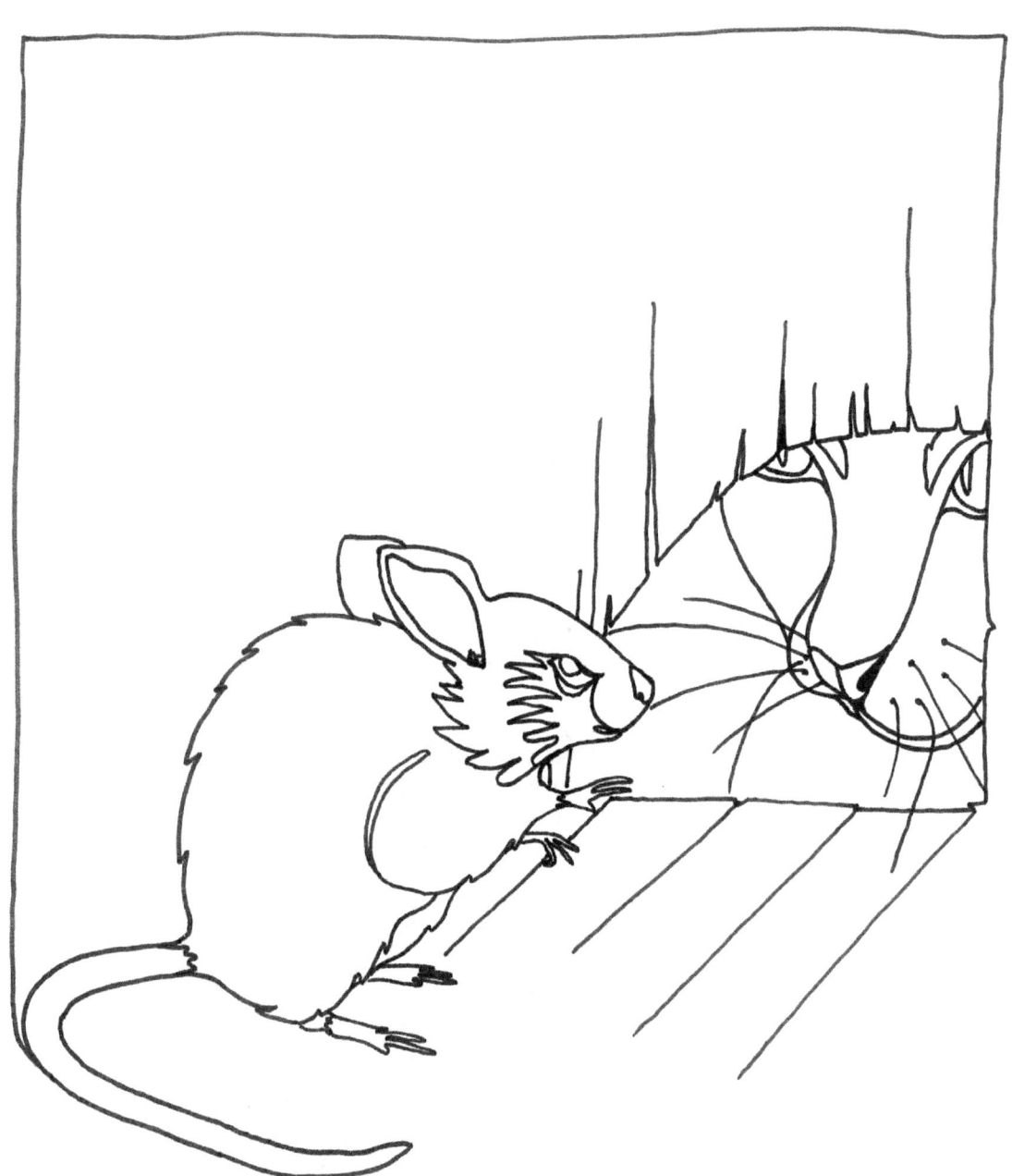

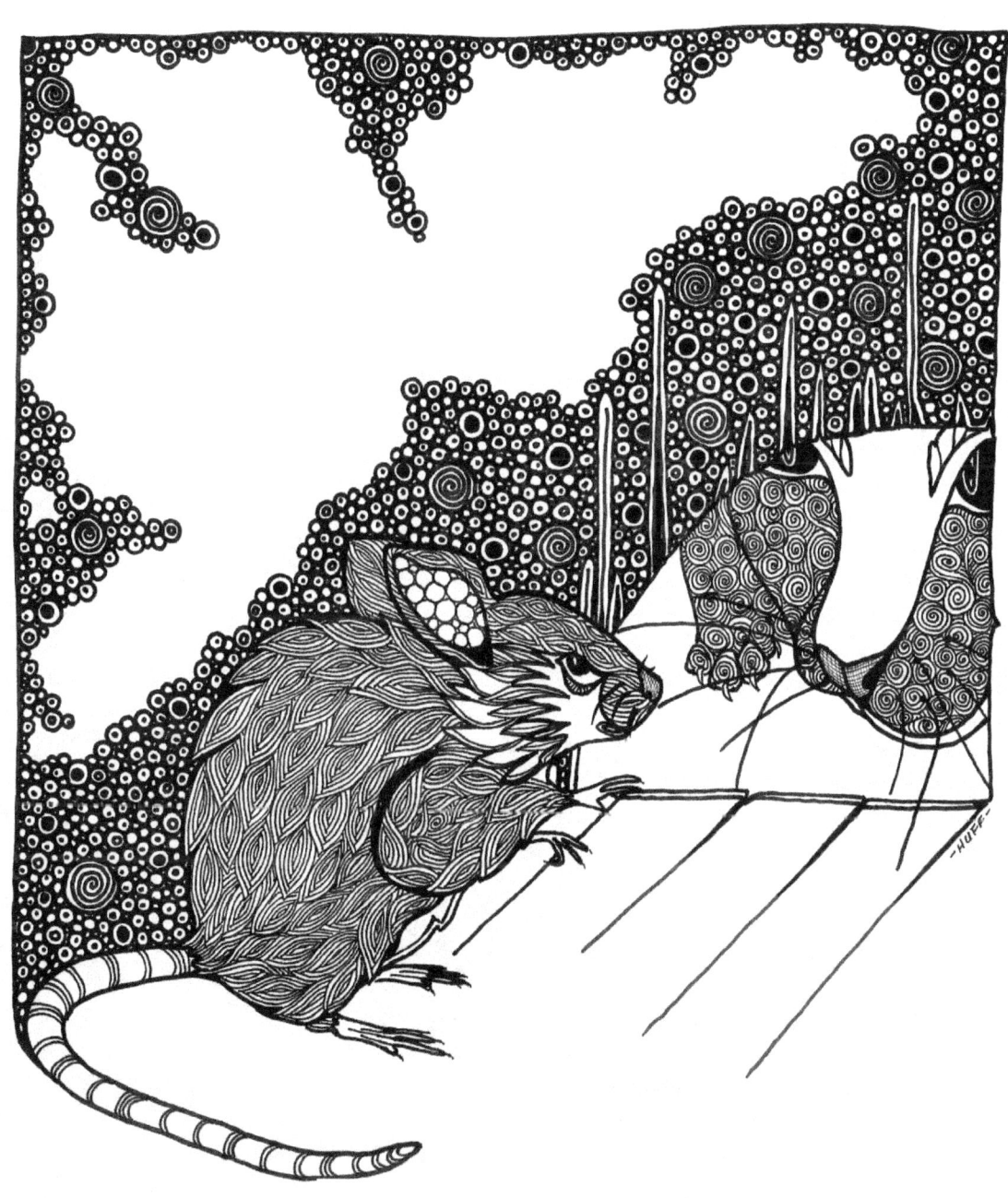

Hiding Mouse

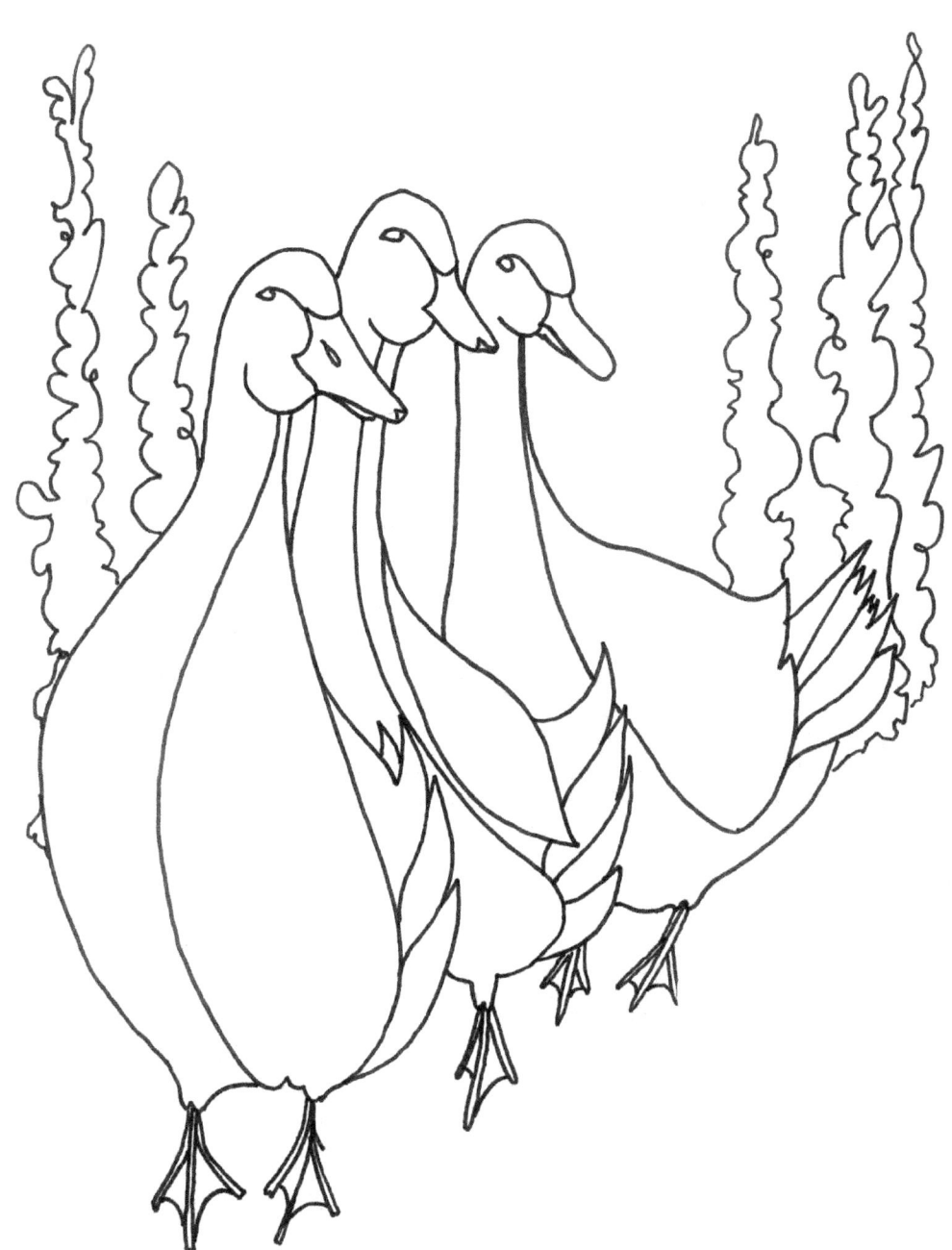

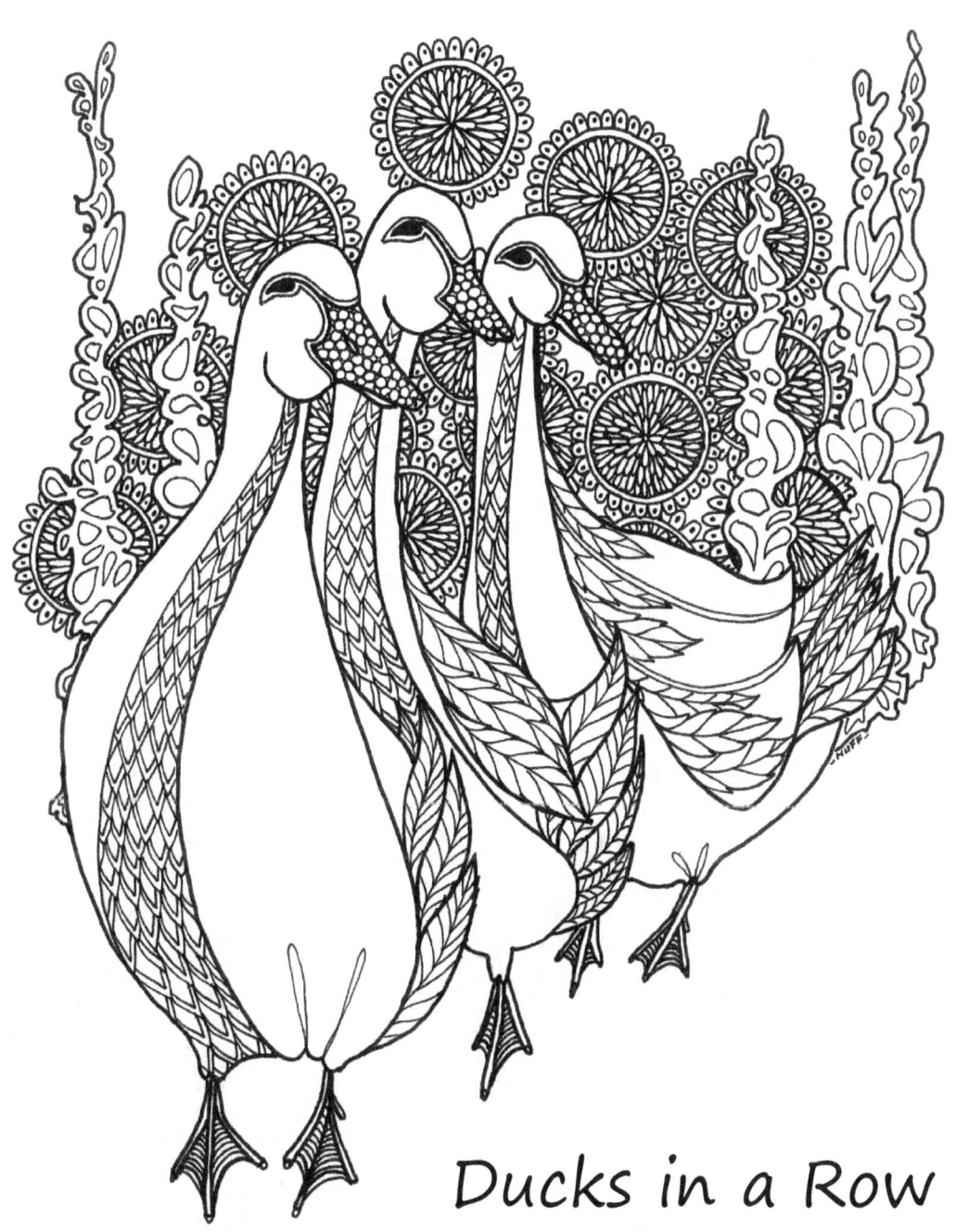

Ducks in a Row

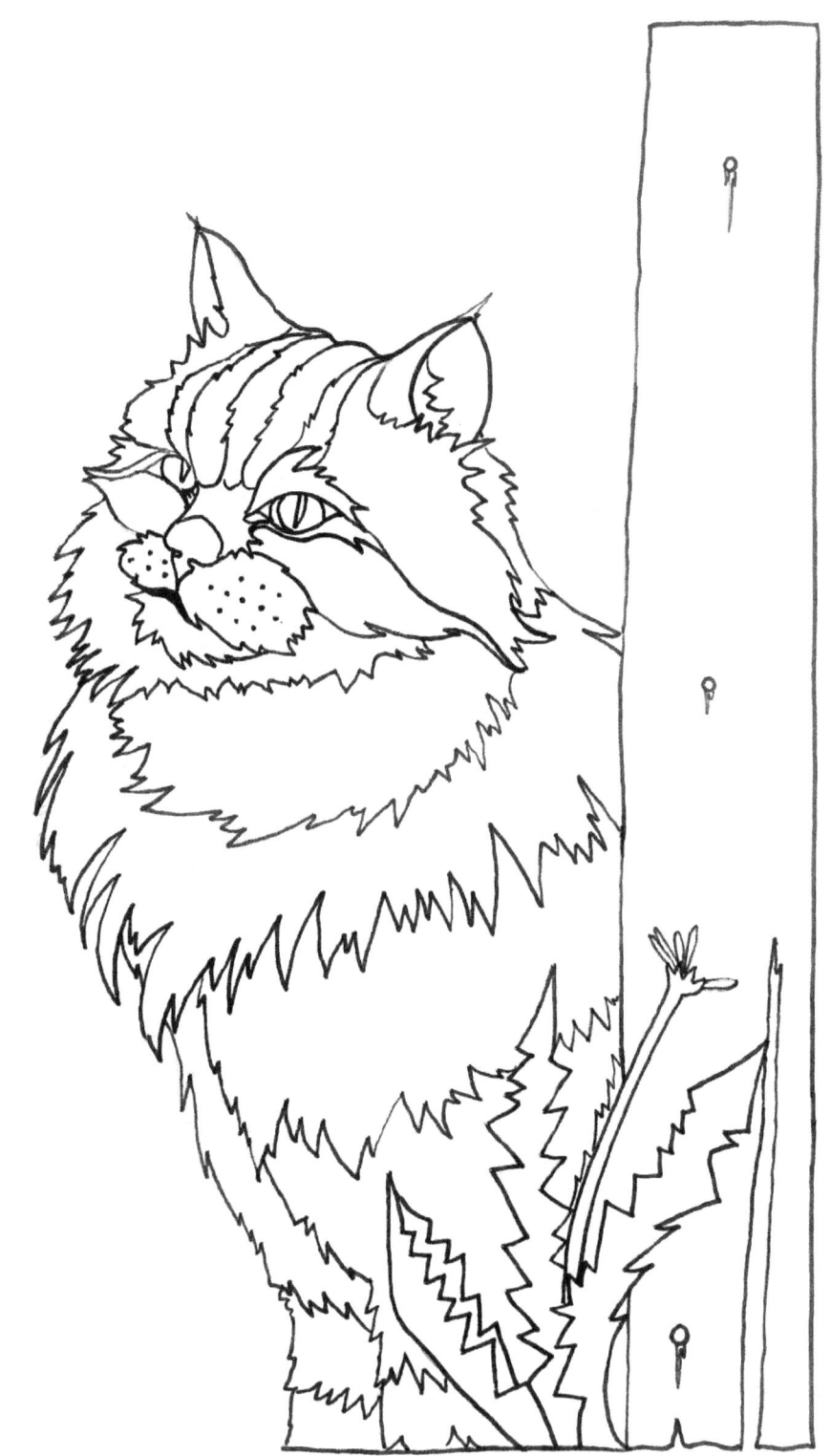

Barn Cat

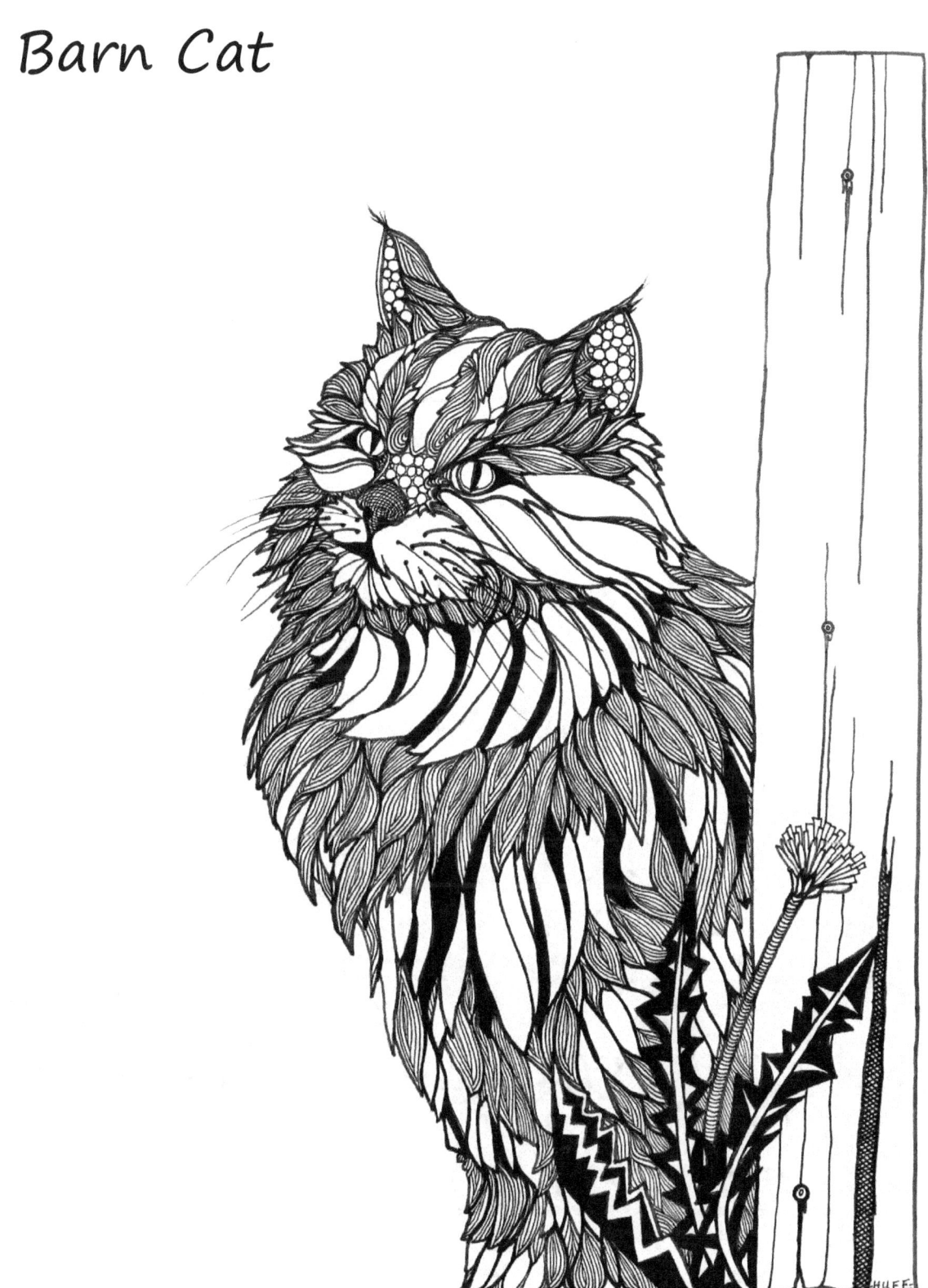

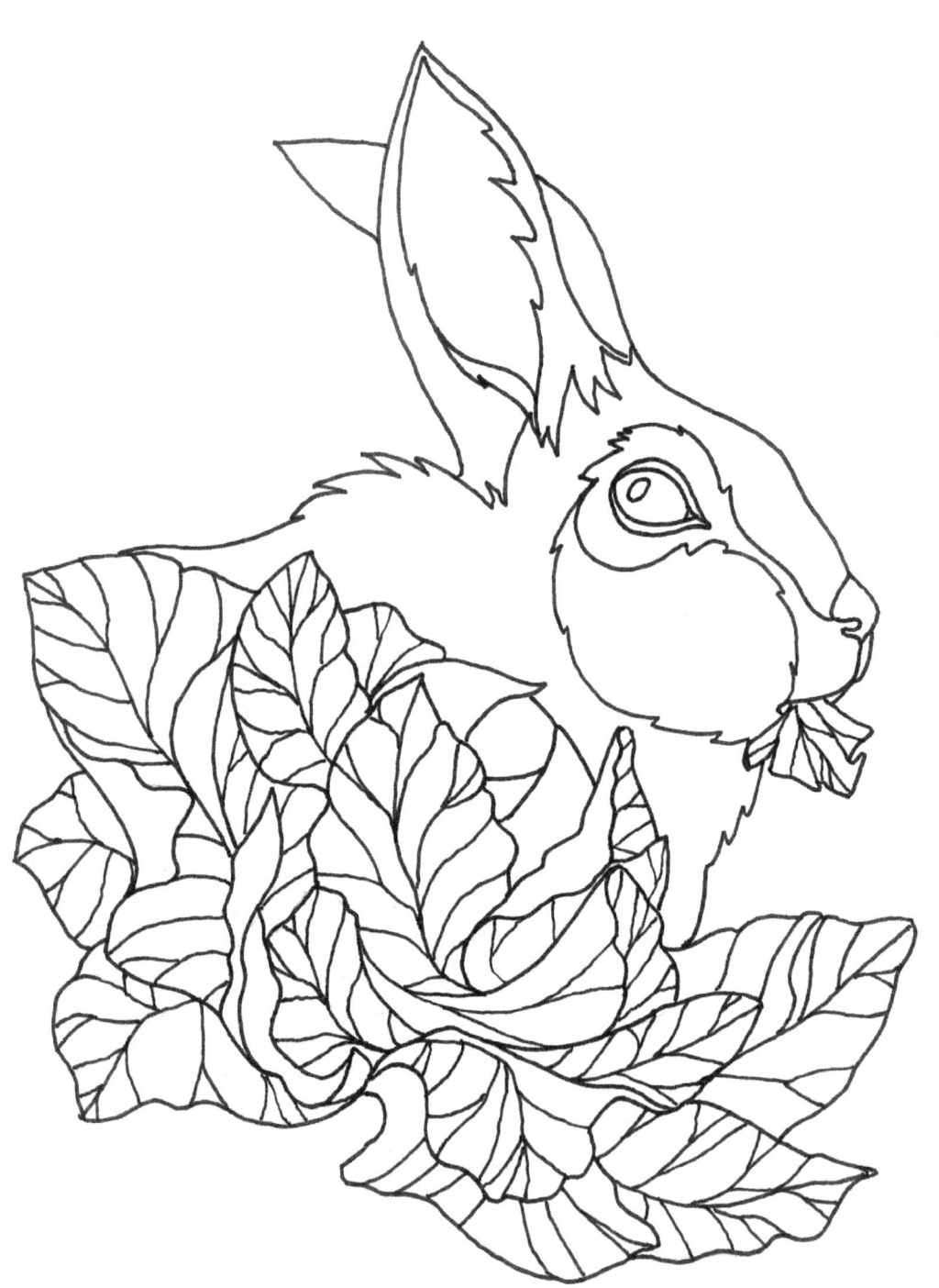

Garden Bunny

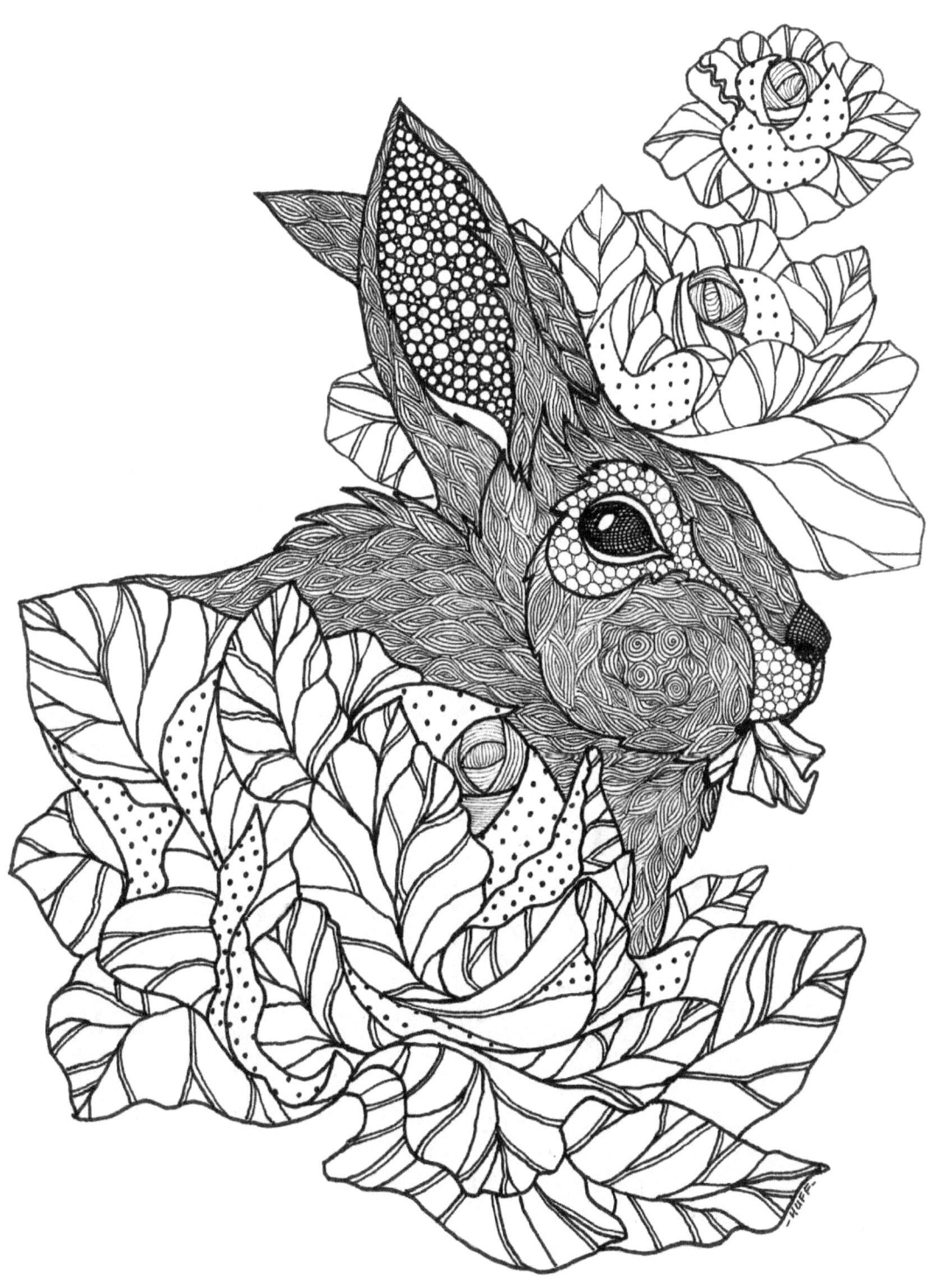

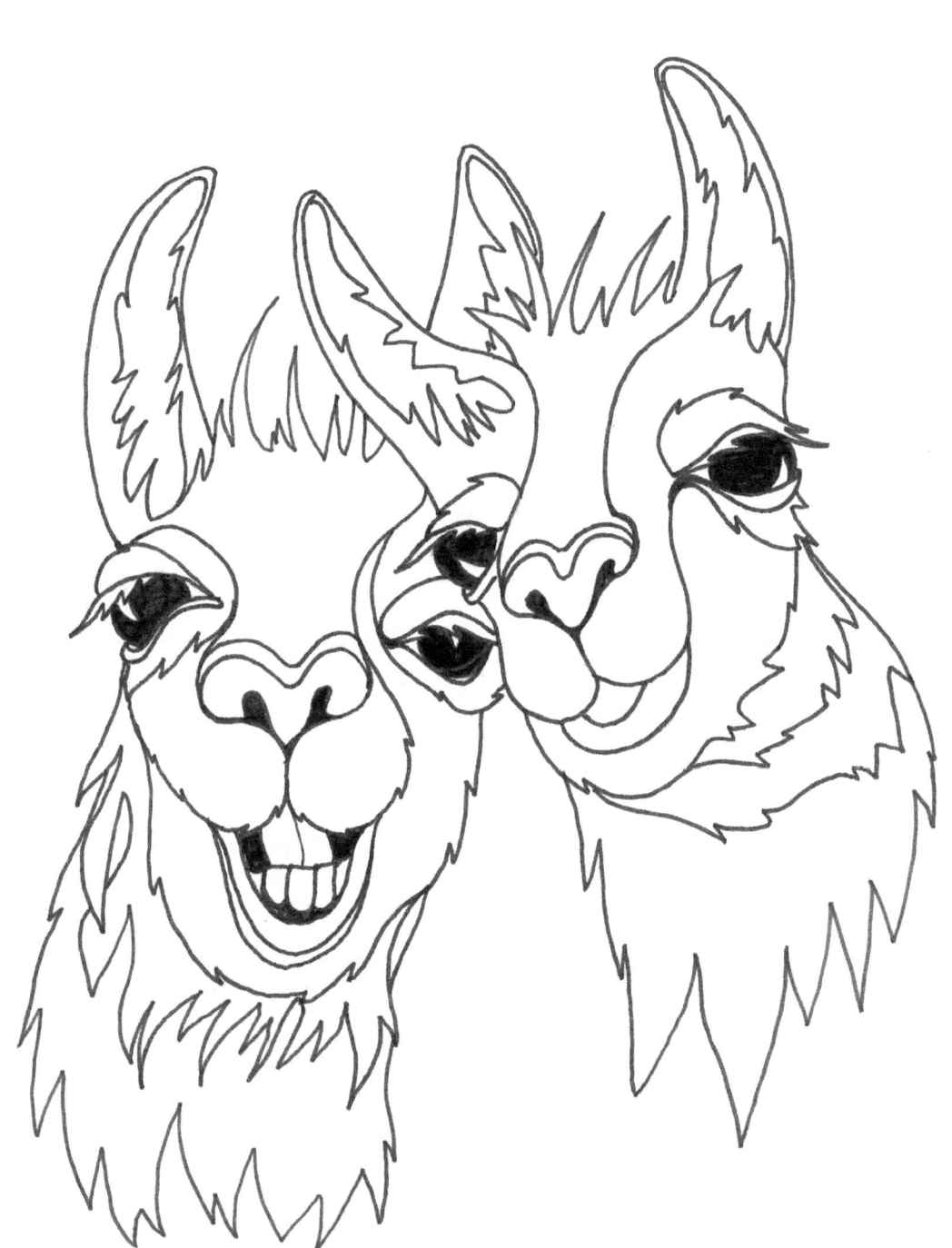

Llama Brothers

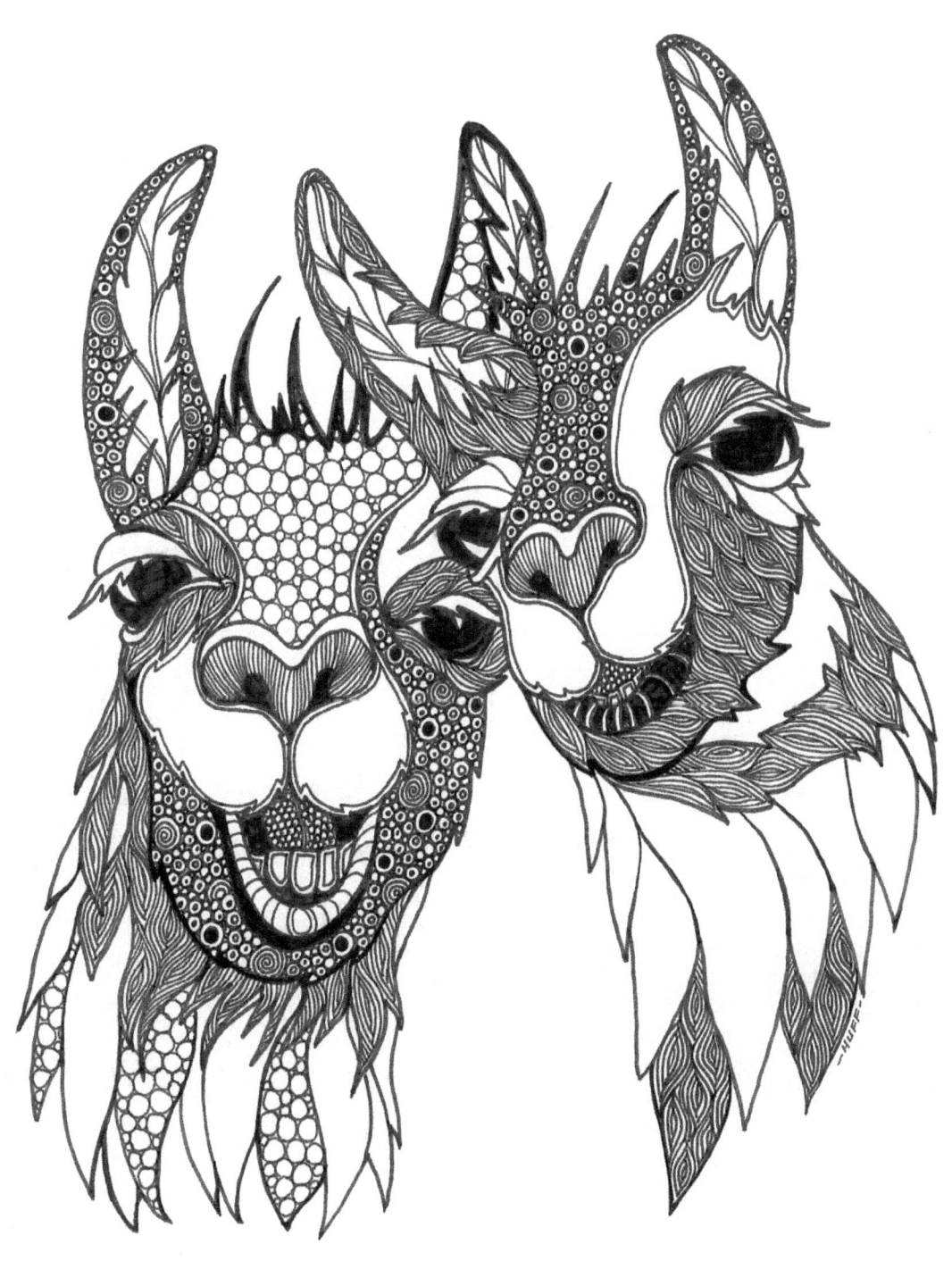

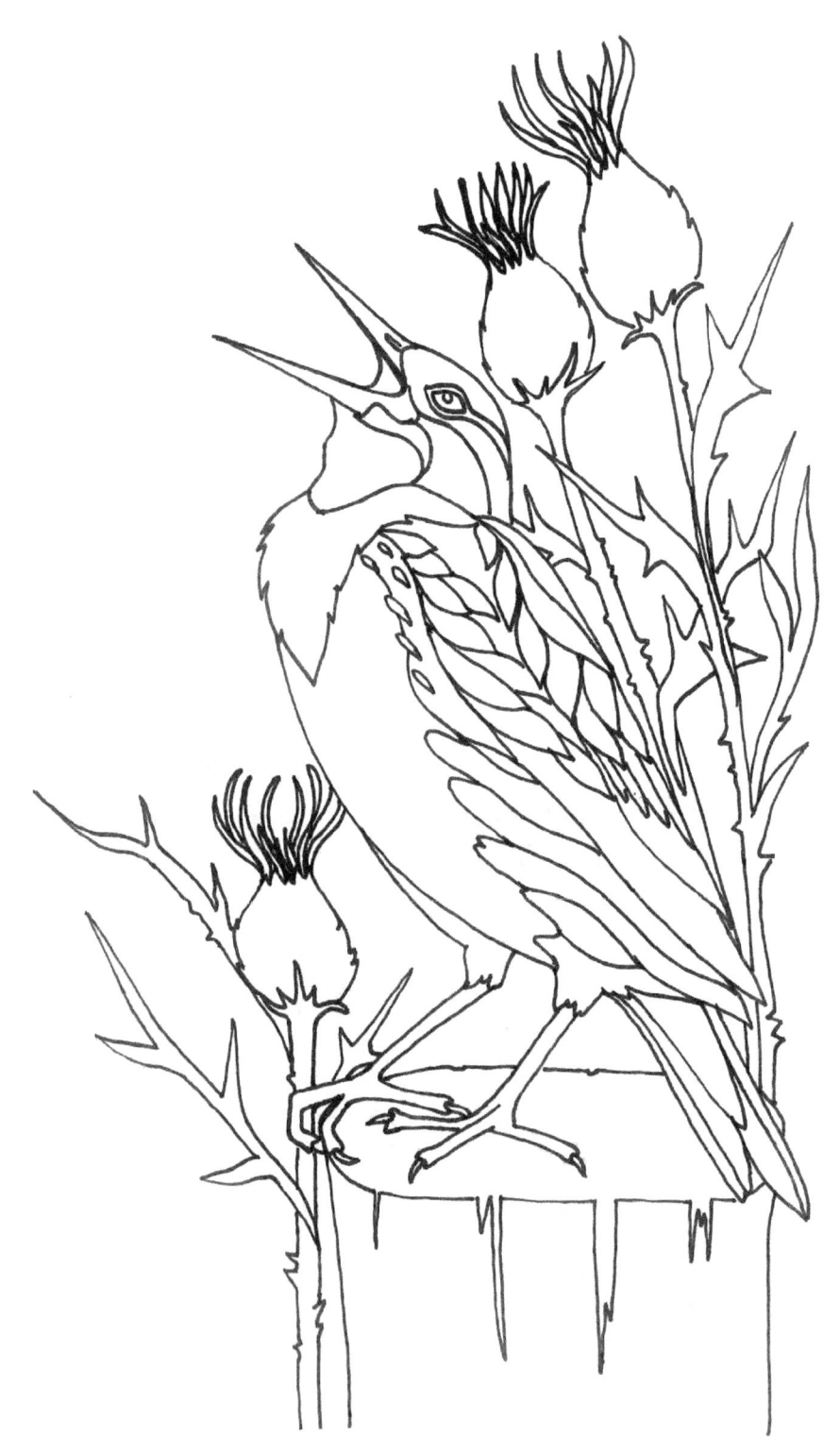

Meadowlark Music

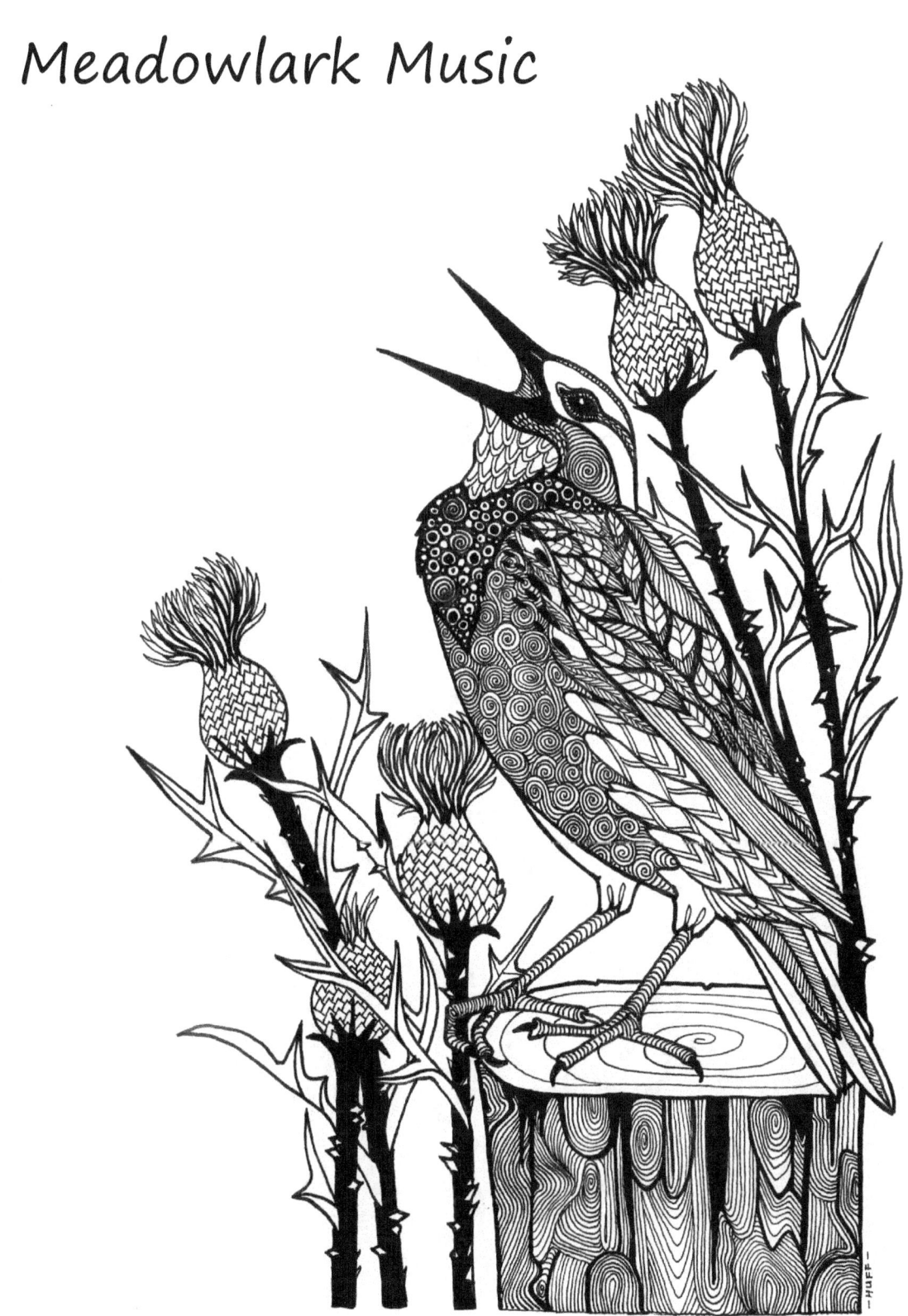

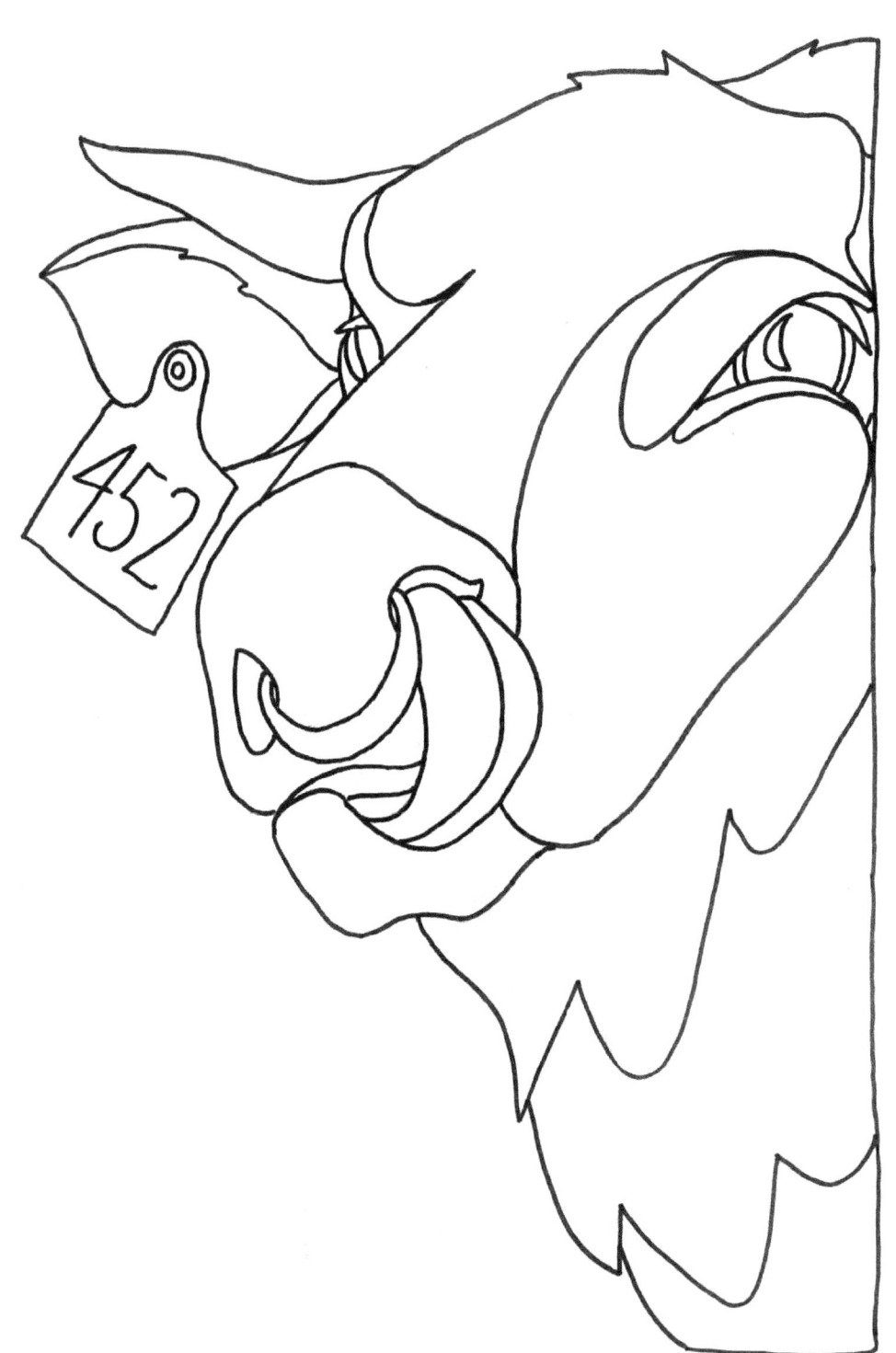

Big Bull

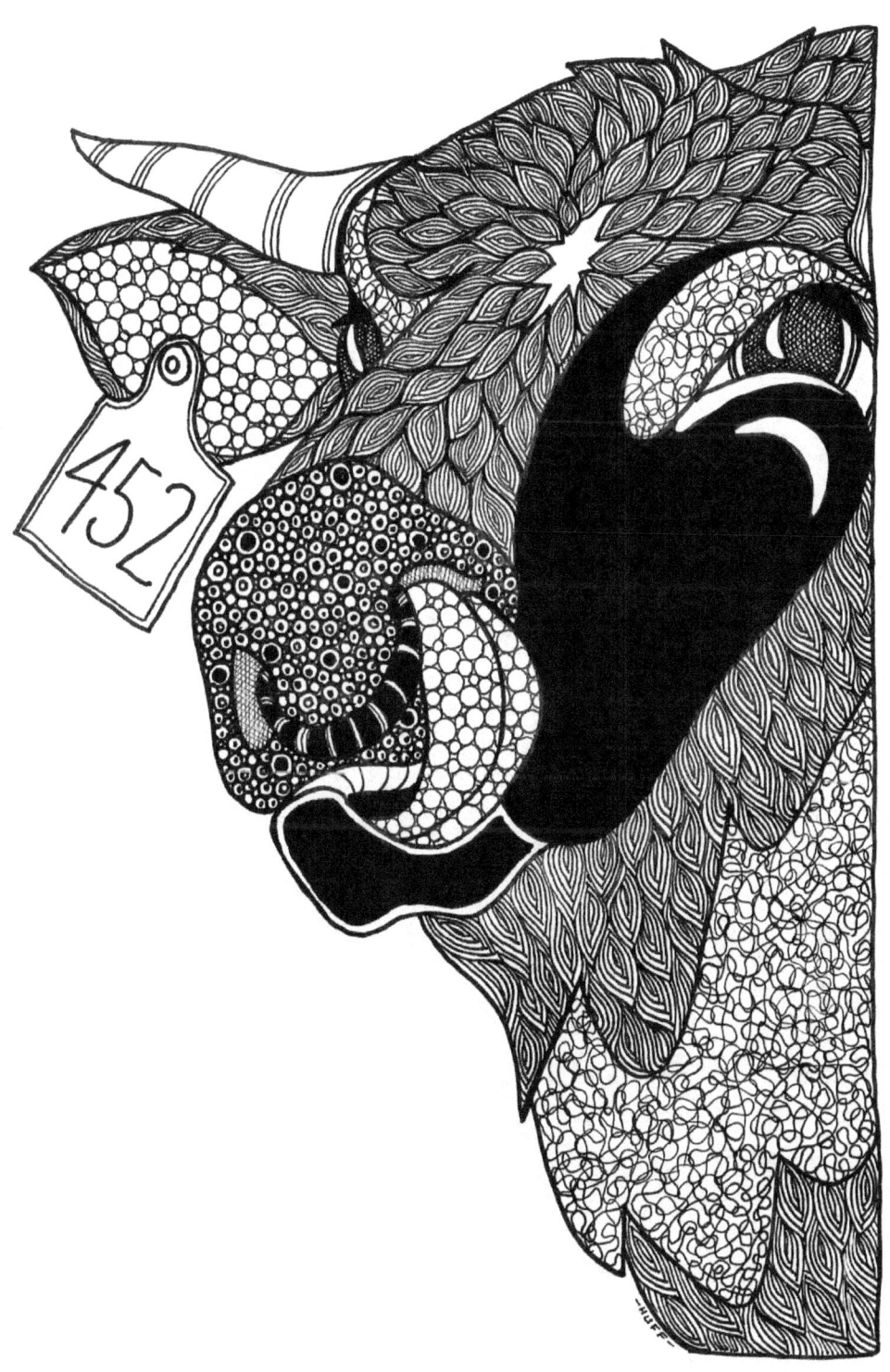

www.ingramcontent.com/pod-product-compliance
Lightning Source LLC
Chambersburg PA
CBHW062208220526
45470CB00009B/2974